Like Winning the Lottery
How Moving to an Island Paradise made me Happier than a Millionaire & How I'm Loving Life as an Expat

by
Greg Pasden

Preview

"Do they know each other?" I wonder if Island Mommy's husband is watching.

Then the unexpected happens. She pulls him to her lips! She's **kissing** him!

"Oh My God!" I mouth. And once again, my mouth falls open in disbelief. Maybe it's not disbelief. Maybe it's more like pure shock because it's a 'Beauty and The Beast' moment! Then she kisses him again. "Oh my God!" I whisper. But this time I think *he* heard me. Because as my mouth is hanging open... he looks over, he smiles... and winks.

Shaking my head in denial and trying not to stare, I watch her help his large, waterlogged form from the pool and into his chair. My staring must be obvious, because he looks over at me and winks again.

She towels him off. "I'm going back in the water Honey," she says. But before she trots back to the pool, she kisses him passionately on the mouth (I think they are putting on a show for me). "Wow!" I mouth. And he sees me staring over my Pina colada again... We make direct eye contact.

"G'Day mate! I guess you discovered our little secret here."

Quickly I look behind me to see if he's talking to someone else, but I'm the only person at the pool.

"Are you talking to me?" I ask embarrassed.

"You must be an American. I can tell by your accent. That explains why you wouldn't know about our little secret. We Ozzies (Australians) have known about this little secret lifestyle for years. What you see is nothing unusual. It's quite normal. This is how we live our every day lives here in paradise. We live like happy millionaires."

"If you don't mind me asking, did you win the lottery? How did you get so lucky?"

"You're a funny man, mate. I quit my job years ago. Then I moved here because the people are genuinely wonderful. Life is filled with music, laughter, happiness, and a foreigner like me are living like kings. Here you'll run out of month before you'll run out of money."

"Are those your children?" I asked with a surprised tone.

"You are a funny man, mate. Of course those are my children," he laughs. "It's obvious you aren't familiar with the lifestyle in the Philippines. So let me tell you about life in the Philippines. Here you can:
- Escape the cold winters
- Live in a place where life goes by at a slow and beautiful pace
- Escape the 'rat race'
- Be able to afford a maid and a driver
- Wake up in the morning and go to bed every night free of frustration or anxiety over money
- Live healthier and with less stress
- Great personal relationships that are full of love, friendship and true caring for each other
- Find the meaning of Life with people that are loving and happy
- Live where the elderly are treated with respect and dignity
- Start a new life in a tropical paradise
- Live like a king in a tropical paradise
- Retire four as rich and 10 times happier

"So mate, does health, better relationships and more fun sound good to you?"

"Of course it does. Who wouldn't like the lifestyle like you have?"

"Great mate! When are you moving here?"

"Me?" I ask in shock.

"It's obvious you like what you see. I'm not blind. So what are you waiting for? If you wait until you grow old and retire, then you'll be to fragile to enjoy this wonderful lifestyle. Bring your wife. She'll love it. Spas, a full time maid, tailors, fresh food, a fun lifestyle in the tropical sun."

"I'm not married."

"Then, like I said, What are you waiting for? When will you join us here in the Philippines?"

At that moment time slowed. I wasn't sure if it was from the potent rum in my pina colada, or if it was from the endorphins and the rapid firing synapses in my brain. But at that moment, thousands of scenarios, thoughts, opinions and questions raced through my mind. What will my friends and family say? Where will I live? How can I make this work?

And then time returned to normal, and I noticed him smiling at me. Then I thought, "It's my life. Why not? Why should I wait for retirement? Why should I let life and opportunity pass me by? Why should I wait another day to find happiness?" So I answer him.

"Today. Today is the day. Today I'm moving to the Philippines. Today I'm starting my happy new life in Paradise."

Dear Mom and Dad,

There comes a time in life, when you walk away from all the drama and people who create it. I decided to surround myself with people who make me laugh, forget the bad, and focus on the good. I love the people who treat me right, and I pray for the ones who don't. Life is too short to be anything but happy.

Falling down is part of life, but getting up is living.

Love, your son,
Greg

PS - When your ready, just leave everything behind, and join me in Paradise.

Foreword

Like Winning the Lottery shares the celebration of risking it all for the dream of a happier life on a tropical island paradise.

Greg Pasden shares what it's like to start a new life, chasing his dreams, and becoming an expat in the Philippines. Along the way he learns how life can be so much richer, exciting and happier. So much so, it's like winning the lottery, and the island lifestyle has made Greg happier than a millionaire.

Enjoy the humorous and witty stories and you'll learn why the Philippines is one of the top ranked happiest places on earth— and learn how the Philippines is one of the friendliest countries for being an expat.

Are you thinking of escaping the rat race, quitting your job and retiring early, living the ultimate lifestyle on a tropical island? If the answer is *yes*, then you'll enjoy...

Like Winning the Lottery
How Moving to an Island Paradise made me
Happier than a Millionaire &
How I'm Loving Life as an Expat

Dedication

I'm dedicating this book to my wife Rose. She has been my inspiration for writing this book. I love the way you make me laugh, the way you make me happy, and the way you make me see all the funniness in the world we live in.

As the whine of the jet engines are spooling down...

"Air Conditioning?"

..."OFF"

"External Power?"

..."ON"

"Battery Power Switch?"

..."OFF"

"Voice Recorder Circuit Breaker?"

..."IN. Shutdown Secure Checklist - COM-PLETE"

"Great flight Lyle!"

"You too, Greg."

"Thanks my friend."

"What's *your* plan today?"

"I'm sure everyone is partied out from all the New Year's Eve parties last night. So I'm thinking about just hanging out at the pool after I catch up on my sleep. That was a long flight last night."

"Sleep when you die my young friend. Go check into your hotel room, put your swim suit on and meet me at the pool for Pina Coladas. This Filipino hotel makes the best Pina Coladas on the planet... and what makes them better is that it's my treat. You'll thank me later. And if you get to the pool first, start ordering the pina coladas without me."

"Aye, Aye! You're the Captain."

Twenty minutes later, Lyle and I check into the hotel on what was once Clark Air Force Base. Clark Air Force Base was the home to the grandest Air Force Base in Asia, and home to thousands of US airmen until November of 1991. That November, the United States didn't renew its lease, so the Air Base was returned to the Philippine government. Today, Clark is an international airport, a manufacturing hub, and it is also bordered by the world famous 'entertainment district' of Angeles City.

"Greg, I'm in my regular room 241. So if you get there before me, do as I said earlier. Start ordering drinks and charge them to my room."

I smile, "Aye, aye."

Minutes later I'm at the pool. A lovely lady escorts me to a padded lounge chair, she spreads out 2 towels for me, and takes my drink order.

"A pina colada, please."

A moment later with my pina colada in hand, I take a deep breath and enjoy the poolside scenery, the blueness of the vivid sky, the intoxicating tropical air, and the relaxing sound of the breeze blowing through the palm trees. It's a much needed cleansing experience for my body and soul. It's really the first time in 53 weeks that I've been able to catch my breath. Why? Because 53 weeks earlier, I got a huge punch the gut.

Let me tell you the story...

53 Weeks Earlier

I'm in the business of aviation. Actually I'm a pilot in the unglamorous world of flying night cargo around the world. Yep, flying boxes instead of people. Don't get me wrong. Flying for a living is a good job with some great benefits - like seeing the world from thirty thousand feet, and watching the moon rise over cities with strange and exotic sounding names - like Qingdao, Pampanga, Shanghai, and Kuala Lumpur. But flying and working 16 hour days around the globe is exhausting, stressful, and hard on anyone's body.

Enough whining about that. So what do I do on my days off from flying night cargo? Well, I'm not really "off". I'm still flying around the world, but as a pilot in the Air National Guard. If only it was 1 week end a month and a 2 week summer camp, but it's not. As a military pilot I'm flying training missions 2 to 3 days each week, plus the additional 30-day operational missions to foreign countries (where people always seem to be shooting at us), plus I'm on call 365 days a year. So how do I describe my current life? I think I'd have to say I'm an exhausted, flying nomad who is running full speed ahead on the proverbial hamster wheel of life... working continuously so I can pay the bills for me and my family.... Day after day after day... Except for tomorrow.

Why not tomorrow?

Tomorrow is Christmas! Thank you Jesus. And I can't wait to get home to be with the family, to see what Santa brought me, and to get some much needed rest. Unfortunately I still have another 4 hours of driving through the night before getting home from work.

Over the River and Through the woods

It's 8pm on Christmas Eve, the radio is playing Christmas carols, and I'm singing right along with them. The singing helps me stay awake during the monochrome drive home. About every 30 minutes or so I'll get a splash of holiday color from the homes that are decorated with traditional Christmas lights. And even though I can't see the fronts of the houses, I still imagine the yards are decorated with plastic Santa's, or a snowmen made by the kids. But since I'm driving in the dark, I can only see the star like shine from the Christmas lights. The twinkling lights make me smile and give me a warm feeling inside... even while I'm freezing in my old Chevy truck.

My old Chevy's seen better days. *"Brrrr, it's cold!"* I wiggle my toes and blow on my fingers while mumbling my favorite winter mantra, "I hate the cold. I hate the cold. I really hate the cold."

In my mind I keep telling myself that I can tolerate this cold, and that I'm almost home. But I really HATE the COLD weather. I *REALLY* hate it!

... and as I'm chanting, my favorite Christmas song by Bing Crosby begins to play, and it brings me back to the Christmas spirit...

*"Mele Kalikimaka is the thing to say
on a bright Hawaiian Christmas Day.
That's the island greeting that we send to you
From the land where palm trees sway.
Here we know that Christmas will be green and bright.
The sun to shine by day and all the stars at night.
Mele Kalikimaka is Hawaii's way to say Merry Christmas to you"*

... And my cell phone rings. I recognize this number. Being in the jolly Christmas spirit I answer,

"Merry Christmas! I'm only 4 hours away..."

Now even though I don't want you to imagine this, I'm going to ask you to *imagine this.*

I'm holding my cell phone to my ear, I'm still driving my heater-less truck, it's Christmas Eve and...

... I learn I no longer have 2 cars in the garage. I no longer have a garage. I no longer have a home to go home to. I no longer have money in the bank. Instead the only things that I have now are my suitcase full of dirty clothes, 3 maxed out credit cards, and my old, cold Chevy pickup truck...

... And I'm starting a life alone. It almost sounds like the makings of a Country Music hit record, but it's not. Instead, I'm getting a divorce.

With my future uncertain, my stomach wrenching, and my throat burning with bile, I pull over to collect my thoughts — before my thoughts come out my mouth and into my lap.

Getting out of the truck, I step to the edge of the road, I fall to my knees, and I start to pray... But instead of praying, I throw up. Not a little. It's the fist in the gut and everything goes.

Whew, not good.

With my mind spinning and my guts spilling into the snow, words finally come out of my mouth. "What am I going to do?"

Several more bouts of gut wrenching agony, and I know I need something to make me feel better. Something to stop my head from spinning. Not a drink though. I need something stronger. Something more powerful. I need my Dad.

So back in the old, cold Chevy. I point the truck in the right direction and I start driving.

Is there any room at the Inn?

"Hello, anyone home?" I call out as I walk in my parents house. It's close to midnight and I don't want my parents to mistake me for Santa Claus or worse — a burglar. Mom and Dad have plenty of guns in the house, so I want to make sure they know it's me.

"Woof! Woof! Woof!"

"Hi *'Silly', don't you recognize me? Stop barking or you'll scare Mom and Dad.*"

'Silly' is the name of my parents' black labrador retriever. Dad named her Silly because he said, "Silly sounds better than naming her 'Damn-It'." Dad would tease us saying, "Can you imagine how awful it would sound if the neighbors heard me calling for a dog named Damn-it? Damn-It, get over here!" This is why I named her Silly. Dad always had a unique sense of humor.

"Greg? Is that you? What are you doing here? It's so late... or is it early?"

"Merry Christmas Dad," I try to smile. "Can we talk?"

"Of course we can. We can always talk. Do you want a Christmas cookie?"

"That would be nice. I need anything to get this awful taste out of my mouth. Do you have any milk?"

"Here you go. I know you like the frosted Santa cookies."

"Thanks Dad."

"Now tell me... what's so important that you needed to come here at O-dark-early to talk to your Dad? You look like you just ate a crap sandwich. Come to think of it, it smell like you ate one too."

With frayed nerves and a shaky voice, I tell my father everything that happened. I can see he shares my pain. Dad has always been a good empathizer.

Looking at me, and taking a deep breath, Dad does something so uncommon for him. He walks over to me, he hugs me, and he says, "I love you son."

Upon hearing these unfamiliar words spoken by my father, I choke up. I even think one my eye balls is beginning to sweat. (At least that's what I'm calling it. A sweaty eye ball).

After what seems like a long minute, Dad says, "Enough of this hugging stuff. Do you want to stay here tonight? You can sleep in your sister's old room. We fixed it up with a doll theme since your sister and Mom have so many old dolls. Oh, and don't worry about sleeping here. I won't tell anyone you sleeping with your sister's dolls."

We both laugh a little.

"Maybe after you get some sleep, and a belly full of your mother's home cooking you'll feel a little better."

With a smile, and a lump in my throat, I say, "That would be nice."

Where's the Sandman when you need him?

As you can imagine, sleep is avoiding me. Not because I'm trying to stay awake and listen for the sound of reindeer landing on my parents roof, or for Santa Claus to come sliding down the chimney. I'm sad, I'm unhappy, and I have lots of questions dancing through my head — when it should be sugar plums.

Being unhappy is really an anomaly for me. I'm always an optimist. I'm always motivating others, I'm enthusiastic, and I'm a happy person. So for me to be sad or unhappy, this is not normal. It feels terrible.

Then for some reason I remember a scene from the movie "Pan" where Peter Pan tells his friends that if **they** want to fly, then all they had to do is think of **their** 'Happy Thought'. With their 'Happy Thought' they can do 'most anything'... including flying. Tonight I'm hoping that a happy thought will help me sleep.

But what is my 'Happy Thought'? It's not a Corvette... or one million dollars (although a million dollars would have made me feel a little better)... or the German fashion model Heidi something (I wish she could make me feel better, but I'm guessing she'd end up with the million dollars). Then I remember **my Happy Thought**. It's when I was a contestant on 'The Dating Game' in college, and I was asked...

..."Thank you contestant number one".

"Contestant number two... Describe to Miss Ohio what would make you happy."
"Uhhhh.... Partying all night in Vegas with unlimited shots of Jaeger... Uhhhh.... Winning a thousand dollars at black jack, and.... Uhhhh then partying all night until dawn! Am I Right? Yeah, party on Dudes!"

And the audience cheers.

While contestant number 2 revels at his own answer, I wonder 2 things:

1. Will this moron find more than 2 brain cells so he can get a job? and
2. Why doesn't he imagine winning a million dollars instead of only a thousand dollars?

Anyway... It's my turn to answer the question...

"Contestant number three. Describe to Miss Ohio what would make you happy."

"Miss Ohio, what would make me happy would definitely involve being on a tropical island, lots of palm trees, cool ocean breezes, and my toes enjoying the warm, talcum white sand. I would start with a sunrise walk on the beach. Then I'd spend a few hours riding waves. After that I'd have breakfast with the local fishermen on the beach where we'd be eating fresh fish, fruit and drinking rich coffee while listening to the wild life in the nearby jungle. In the afternoon I'd be snorkeling followed by an outdoor shower under a waterfall so I could feel the warm sun on me while looking out at the ocean. That afternoon I'd meet up with the fisherman to find a delicious yellow fin tuna that I'd grill it on an open fire on the beach. Then you and I would spend the evening laying on the beach near the fire, look at the stars and listening to the ocean."

Contestant number two: "Dude, that's too-o-o-o complicated.... Just go to Vegas with me Baby!!!" And the crowd roars — at the imbecile.

Announcer: "Thank you contestants for your answers. And the winner is..."

...In reality, it doesn't matter who won the date with the gorgeous Miss Ohio. What really matters is that I learned more about myself that night, and that I remember what makes me happy. Being on a tropical island, near the ocean, and experiencing island life. This is *my happy thought*. This is what I **need** in my life. I **need** happiness. I want a life on the beach. I want a life in the warm tropical sun... with the palm trees... and everything that comes with it. I know my *Happy Thought*...

And finally with this Happy Thought, I'm beginning to have visions. Visions of sugar plums dancing in my head.

Let's get Back to the Pool - in The Philippines - under the Warm Morning Sun

"Sir, is there anything I can do for you?"

"Another pina colada would be nice."

"As you wish, sir."

While watching the lovely form of the waitress walk away to get me another tropical concoction, I get distracted (which is hard to do since I'm enjoying watching the pretty waitress). But laughter along with getting splashed from the people in the pool was enough to get my attention. The splashing in the pool is coming from an older husky, foreign guy, and he appears to be his grandchildren. Seeing them splashing, having fun and being happy makes me wonder if I'll ever be able to have a happy life again. Nevertheless, their happiness is contagious, and I find myself smiling.

"Excuse me sir. Here is your pina colada," and like that, I have another reason to smile.

Mmm, these fresh, frozen concoctions are magical.

"Mommy! Mommy, come join us!" and my attention is drawn back to the pool. As I look over my pina colada, my jaw drops to my chest. Wow! "Mommy" doesn't look like any mommy I've ever seen before. This "Mommy" is a 'hotty'. Beautifully tanned, long hair, shapely and bikini clad. And as I blatantly ogle, she dives into the water to join her happy kids. They play and laugh together, and once again I find myself with an uncontrollable smile. I guess happiness really is contagious.

Enjoying the warmth of the sun and spying over my delicious fruity drink, I watch the beautiful island "Mommy" begin to swim. Swimming away from her kids. And as I admire her beautiful form in the water, I wonder where her husband is. Hopefully he's not watching me admiring his wife.

"Wow, she looks gorgeous," I say to myself just before something bizarre happens in the water. Beautiful Island Mommy begins swimming toward the chubby, old, foreign guy. Then she does something that completely dumbfounds me. She swims up behind the old, chubby, foreign guy and wraps her arms around his neck and pushes him under water! Startled, the old guy splashes, resurfaces and turns around to face his assailant. Then he smiles.

"Do they know each other?" I wonder if Island Mommy's husband is watching.

Then the unexpected happens. She pulls him to her lips! She's **kissing** him!

"Oh My God!" I mouth. And once again, my mouth falls open in disbelief. Maybe it's not disbelief. Maybe it's more like pure shock because it's a Beauty and the Beast moment! Then she kisses him again. "Oh my God!" I whisper. But this time I think *he* heard me. Because as my mouth is hanging open... he looks over, he smiles... and winks.

Shaking my head in denial and trying not to stare, I watch her help his large, waterlogged form from the pool and into his chair. My staring must be obvious, because he looks over at me and winks again.

She towels him off. "I'm going back in the water Honey," she says. But before she trots back to the pool, she kisses him passionately on the mouth (I think they are putting on a show for me now). "Wow!" I mouth. And he sees me staring over my Pina colada again... We make direct eye contact.

"G'Day mate! I guess you discovered our little secret here."

Quickly I look behind me to see if he's talking to someone else, but I'm the only person at the pool.

"Are you talking to me?" I ask embarrassed.

"You must be an American. I can tell by your accent. That explains why you wouldn't know about our little secret. We Ozzies (Australians) have known about this little secret lifestyle for years. What you see is nothing unusual. It's quite normal. This is how we live our every day lives here in paradise. We live like happy millionaires."

"If you don't mind me asking, did you win the lottery? How did you get so lucky?"

"You're a funny man, mate. I quit my job years ago. Then I moved here because the people are genuinely wonderful. Life is filled with music, laughter, happiness, and a foreigner like me are living like kings. Here you'll run out of month before you'll run out of money."

"Are those your children?" I asked with a surprised tone.

"You are a funny man, mate. Of course those are my children," he laughs. "It's obvious you aren't familiar with the lifestyle in the Philippines. So let me tell you about life in the Philippines."

Here you can:

• Escape the cold winters
• Live in a place where life goes by at a slow and beautiful pace
• Escape the 'rat race'
• Be able to afford a maid and a driver
• Wake up in the morning and go to bed every131131 night free of frustration or anxiety over money
• Live healthier and with less stress

- Great personal relationships that are full of love, friendship and true caring for each other
- Find the meaning of Life with people that are loving and happy
- Live where the elderly are treated with respect and dignity
- Start a new life in a tropical paradise
- Live like a king in a tropical paradise
- Retire twice as rich and 10 times happier

"So mate, does health, better relationships and more fun sound good to you?"

"Of course it does. Who wouldn't like the life-style like you have?"

"Great mate! When are you moving here?"

"Me?" I ask in shock.

"It's obvious you like what you see. I'm not blind. So what are you waiting for? If you wait until you grow old and retire, then you'll be to fragile to enjoy this wonderful lifestyle. Bring your wife. She'll love it. Spas, a full time maid, tailors, fresh food, a fun lifestyle in the tropical sun."

"I'm not married."

"Then, like I said, What are you waiting for? When will you join us here in the Philippines?"

At that moment time slowed. I wasn't sure if it was from the potent rum in my pina colada, or if it was from the endorphins and the rapid firing synapses in my brain. But at that moment, thousands of scenarios, thoughts, opinions and questions raced through my mind. What will my friends and family say? Where will I live? How can I make this work?

And then time returned to normal, and I noticed him smiling at me. Then I thought, "It's my life. Why not? Why should I wait for retirement? Why should I let life and opportunity pass me by? Why should I wait another day to find happiness?" So I answer him.

"Today. Today is the day. Today I'm moving to the Philippines. Today I'm starting my happy new life in Paradise."

Pilot Vests + T-Shirts + Yahoo Messenger = A Budding Relationship

As pilots, we need to be professional in the face of dangerous and stressful situations every time we get in the jet. But to offset the stress and dangers we face, we always seem to be joking around or poking fun at one another and ourselves. One example is wearing silly footy pajamas in the cockpit (on long flights). Or attaching a red strobe light to their hat so that it flashes while doing the exterior pre-flight inspection. My buddy's reasoning for this is, "Since we work in the dark of night, this crazy hat makes me more visible and easier to see. It helps keep me safe." Well, his idea was a premonition of things to come.

Have you ever seen the construction workers on the side of the road? Did you notice that they are wearing neon-reflective vests? The idea behind bright vest is the same as my buddy's — it makes you visible to keep you safe.

Guess what? The airline industry got that same idea and decided that all pilots should wear the handsome, reflective, bright colored vests anytime we are not inside the jet. When I think about it, it makes us look like groupies for the punk rock band, DEVO. Ugh, what a terrible thought.

Anyway, one night we are in flight operations doing our pre-flight planning, when one of our pilots struts in the room wearing a custom T-shirt painted to look just like our uniform shirts **including** the neon vest. Everyone gets a laugh — even the strict managers.

"Hey, Greg. I hear your moving to Angeles City in the PI. Can you do me a favor?"

John asks me if I can get 100 of them made for him. I agree, so he tells me where he had his made.

Three weeks later I arrive to my new home in Angeles City and I have no idea where to stay. To make things simple, I decide to stay in what looks like a highway travel lodge. But that's not what I discovered when I walked inside. Inside the staff are friendly, the service is great, and they even provide an inexpensive transportation service around the local area. After I check in, I'm hoping to take advantage of the transportation service in hopes that I'll find the custom T-shirt shop — because I forgot where my buddy told me he had them made. Yikes.

Seeing the concierge, I ask "Excuse me, do you know where they make custom T-shirts? I want to have 100 made."

"Yes, sir. Our driver will be happy to drive you there."

After a brief wait, driver Dan pulls up.

"To the beach, sir Greg?"

"I wish Dan, but not today. I'm actually looking for a place to make me a 100 custom T-shirts." Giving Dan the few details I can remember, he assures me he knows where to go.

Twenty minutes later we pull into what I can assume is a parking area for a run down looking wooden building. "Dan, this seems like a strange place to make custom shirts".

"Not to worry Sir Greg. This is where you want to be. Trust me."

Being a stranger in a foreign country, what do I know. Maybe this is how they do business here.

We arrange a pickup time, and I tip Dan before I walk across the parking lot towards the **only** door I can find... And I'm surprised at what I find. It's **not** a custom shirt shop at all. It is a modern industrial sewing factory. I guess I shouldn't judge the building by its cover. So I walk inside.

As the heavy metal door closes behind me — and locks - a very small person glances up from behind her sewing machine, and makes eye contact with me. She smiles at me and immediately goes back to work. But as she's working, she keeps glancing up at me and smiling... except this time she winks. Suddenly her machine stops. Something is wrong because she looks very upset. Removing what looks like the sewing needle from the machine, she gets up and walks near me to get a replacement needle... and I think she looks so adorable.

Long black hair pulled back in a pony tail, big brown eyes, high cheek bones, and the most beautiful and inviting smile. (I think I just described 20 million Filipino girls.)

"Excuse me, miss. Can you help me?"

"I'm sorry sir, I cannot help anyone. I am *only* a sewing girl, and I am busy... and I just broke my sewing needle. See... and this is going to come out of my salary... and today is not a good time for me to answer questions... and I need to get back to work...I have to make quota."

Quickly she finds a replacement needle, and hurries back to her sewing machine.

I follow. "Is this the place that makes custom t-shirts?"

And even though she is busy and obviously stressed, she looks at me with her big brown eyes and gently says, "No sir. We only manufacture men's white t-shirts. This is a factory. No custom orders here. I'm sorry sir. I must work now. I need this job."

She smiles at me again... and winks. I'm captivated by her eyes and her smile... especially her wink! I'm pretty sure she's flirting.

"Can I ask you another question, miss?"

This time she turns and gives me a mildly, annoyed glance. "Sir, I am many, many, many times busy... and I need to make my quota."

"I'd like to ask you another question. Can I take you to dinner, or maybe lunch, or maybe coffee? I'm new to Angeles City. I thought maybe you could help me get to know the area."

"You are a foreigner... and I've heard stories about foreigners... and how can I trust you?" ... she says with an overly dramatic tone. A few giggles from the girls nearby. I guess our little conversation is creating attention. This is made evident because 2 security guards are heading my way. So I talk faster.

"Excuse me miss. Is being a 'foreigner' a good thing... or a bad thing? Anyway, my name is Greg and I'm **'foreigner'... I mean I'm a nice guy.** Really. But if you change your mind, can I give you my email address. Maybe you can email me."

Quickly I scribble my email on the only paper I have — a 100 hundred peso bill — and give it to her. She looks at my email address on the money, and with a laughing smile she says, "Isn't there a saying that says nice guys finish last?". More giggles erupt from the girls as she winks and slips the bill inside her blouse.

At that moment I feel something, but it's not my heart. Instead it's hands on my shoulders.

"Sir, this is a restricted area. You must leave now. We don't want you to become injured... ***do we***?" Understanding their implied meaning, I soon I find myself alone in the parking lot... without her name, without her contact information, and without 100 t-shirts. But I have hope. I trust that the girl with the funny smile and playful wink will contact me. I guess I'll just have to wait for her to make the next move.

The next move, Ugh! I hate this.

My waiting became days. The days became weeks, and no contact. I'm beginning to wonder if this is what women feel like when guys tell them, "I'll call you" ... and then they don't. Nevertheless, I'm beginning to lose hope.

Weeks go by and I'm completely moved to the Philippines, but I'm still looking for an apartment. Why am I still looking for an apartment? It's because I don't really know my way around town, and my only mode of transportation are my feet. So instead of living in an apartment, I find myself staying in a condotel. What is a condotel? A condotel is similar to a hotel room, but bigger. It has a kitchenette, a sitting area, and a bedroom... but it doesn't included daily housekeeping services. The trade-off is that the condotel is cheaper than a hotel, but about the same price an apartment with the utilities and furniture included. But since I really haven't found where I wanted to live (or have any furniture), the condotel is the best option for me.

So one evening while eating dinner in my condotel, I hear "You Got Mail". Actually it didn't say, "You Got Mail". Instead it was a *'PING!'* sound from Yahoo Instant Messenger letting me know that someone is trying to get my attention. Apparently someone wants to chat with me online. The thing is, I really don't know how to chat online. So this will be my first time. So I look at my computer to see who is 'PINGing' me.

" 'Brain-Banyan'? Who in the heck is 'Brain-Banyon'?" So I write, "Do I know you?"

"You met me in the sewing factory a couple of weeks ago."

"Are you the security guard."

"See how you are. You forgot me already :("

"I'm only joking. Yes, I remember you... but I don't know your name."

"It's Rose"

... And like that, our relationship begins. Albeit through the Yahoo Messenger chat room... but this is the twenty-first century, right? So we chat for what seems like hours before we make plans to meet for a first date.

As the weekend approaches for our first date, I'm getting more and more excited... but most of all, I'm getting more and more nervous. I have all the nervous symptoms including butterflies in the stomach, sweaty palms, even sweaty armpits. It's beginning to feel like Im a thirteen year old boy again. Ugh, what a terrible time in life! But I have to remind myself that all these adolescent worries no longer matter. I'm not that thirteen year old boy any more, and I don't have pimples. Instead, I'm a guy who is going to get to know the cute girl with a playful wink.

Arriving at the restaurant 15 minutes early, I make sure I get a good table with a nice view. I'm excited and I want everything to go perfectly so that I make a good impression as a nice guy and not a bad *foreigner*.

Finally the time arrives. I'm looking at the door. She'll be walking throughout at any second. Well, seconds become minutes. Minutes become an hour and still no Rose.

I take a deep breath and I explain to the restaurant manager that I won't need the table after all. He understands and suggests that I wait a few more minutes.

"Why should I wait? It's been over an hour and she still isn't here."

"This is normal. This is called *Filipino Time*. Take the time you said to meet, then add 1 hour and you have *Filipino Time*. Trust me."

So I take a seat at the table. Minutes later, just like he said, Rose walks through the door. She looks stunning. I guess she used the extra hour to make sure she looked beautiful for our first date.

As the evening progresses, we eat, we talk, and she makes me laugh. After dinner she shows me around town... and we even find the place to order the custom t-shirts. At the end of our date she takes me by the hand and pulls me close. And before I know it, she kisses me!

Words cannot express how surprised and happy I feel, but I try.

"Rose, being with you makes me happy. Happier than a billionaire!"

She laughs, smiles and says, "I make you feel like you won the lottery?"

I nod.

"Does this mean you like me?"

I nod again.

"Then can I kiss you again!"

... And so *our* story begins.

[A Note from the author's wife: Rose says she wasn't winking at me. She says she was blinking - Not winking. She was blinking because she had dust in her eyes. I still like to think she was flirting with me :-)]

Courting a Duck

In the Philippines, the locals have another expression for 'dating'. It's called *'courting'*. To me the word courting brings to mind the image of a prince dating a princess... or should I say **courting** a princess. It doesn't matter what it's called because — according to Filipino custom - I am officially courting Rose.

During our courting, I'm learning many things about the Filipino people, as well as about Rose. I'm learning that going out for a walk can be considered a date, or getting BBQ hotdogs on a stick from a street vendor can be a date, and even watching reruns of Filipino boxing can be a date.

I'm also learning that courting might involve having the entire family join us on a date. I know this sounds as old fashioned as the term *courting*, but this is how *traditional* (not from the city) Filipinos get to know their daughter's courtier.

One of the ways they are insisting to get to know me better is for us all to go to a *karaoke club*. Just hearing the word karaoke club makes me cringe. Needless to say, I am extremely reluctant, because the thought of anyone hearing me singing with my croaking voice would guarantee me losing lots of courtier points. But in the Philippines, karaoke is taken very seriously. This is extremely evident because of the vast number of karaoke clubs here, and the way people dress in character when they go to them.

Why is karaoke so popular here? The most popular reason is because Filipinos love to sing. *"Singing makes you happy. Even poor people can sing and become happy. Singing is Life!"*

Another reason is... *"Because people can perform and express their emotions freely through their performance — be it their hidden emotions of joy, despair, passion, love, or just pure happiness - and everyone will cheer for them even if they sing like a duck."*

Well, this evening Rose's family is trying to convince me that singing will help me gain more points with the family if I go to a karaoke club with them. "You'll like it. We drink, we eat, we talk. It's all good. The family will like you more. Trust us."

I have my doubts but I want to make a good impression with Rose's family, so I reluctantly agree to trust this will increase my score on the Filipino family point board.

After a short ride on 4 motorcycles, all 13 of us walk into the club. And it's not what I imagined. Disco lights, hundreds of people, and a stage for the **brave** performers. Whew, I am so glad there are so many people here. This means there won't be time for me to sing. Hehe.

While Rose and her sister's go to the ladies room to freshen up, me and her brothers order margaritas, local food, and listen to the locals sing. But it's not just singing. It's performing. Some of these people should be putting on professional performances.

After a handsome man finishes a spot on rendition of *Faithfully* by Journey, the lights go down, a new singer gets on stage, and it appears to be a little girl. "How cute," I think. Then I realize it's a little girl that **we** know. It's Rose.

"Tonight I want to dedicate this song to a special person in my life. He is here tonight sitting with my family. So I want to sing this song for him. It's called "Bring me to Life" by Evanesance."

The music starts and a powerful voice starts rocking the stage. And the entire karaoke bar on its feet! I laugh. I'm completely at a loss for words. This powerful voice is from Rose! All 4 feet 8 inches of her belts out a powerful performance that sounds like a professional. Her entire performance is getting cheers, and as the ends people are on their feet giving her a standing ovation. It warms my heart, it makes me proud, and makes me wonder — "What else is in this tiny person?" I can't wait to learn more.

But before I get the chance to learn more, I hear the words that paralyze me in my seat. "Now I want to introduce the man who brought me to life. It's Greg Pasden. Come up here. It's your turn to sing. Don't be shy. Don't be afraid?" And dozens of little hands pushed me to the stage.

Petrified. Yep, that is the exact word to describe how I am feeling right now as Rose slips the microphone into my hand. "You'll be fine. Trust me," and she pats me on the butt.

Then the music starts, and I stand frozen looking into the crowded club. It's evident the people in the club are looking at me and wondering, "Why doesn't the awkward foreigner sing?"

Just as I was about to say into the microphone, "This isn't for me," and walk off the stage, I see Rose's gentle, brown eyes. She knows how I feel. She smiles, she blows me and kiss and she mouths something. Her little gesture gives me a spark of encouragement. To trust her. To believe in myself.

Turning to the karaoke jockey, I ask him to restart the song selection. The seconds before the music starts feel like minutes, but when the music starts, I realized there is no turning back. And I begin to sing...
"It's late in the evening,
She's wondering what clothes to wear.

She puts on her make-up
And brushes her long ***black*** hair.
And then she asks me,
'Do I look alright?'
I said my Darling,
You look Wonderful Tonight"

And as I continue to sing the song "Wonderful Tonight" by Eric Clapton,

... the crowd begins to cheer,

...And Rose's eyes begin to water.

Not soon enough, the song thankfully ends and I pass off the microphone to the next performer. Exiting the stage I'm greeted with hugs and cheers from Rose's family. Then Rose comes over and I'm expecting a hug. Instead she punches my arm.

"See how you are? You made me cry," and she hugs me. "I'm so proud of you. You make me so happy."

Thankfully the understanding eyes of Rose gave me the courage to sing. But it wasn't just the courage to sing. She gave me the courage to sing to her. To express my feelings freely... even if I sounded awful.

Now from this simple event — an event that lasted nearly 4 hours and only cost me twenty dollars - I learned something special about Rose, her family and myself. Our simple singing created powerful emotions, unbreakable bonds, and created memorable moments. I also learned that before we do this again, that I need to get a few singing lessons, because Rose said I sing like a duck.

Factory worker - Full Time Student - Repeat

Rose and I have been seeing each other more frequently, and it didn't take me long to realize that I was falling for her... and she's makes it was easy for me. Rose has a great sense of humor, she's adventuresome, she likes traveling, she likes sports, she's well organized, she has a good work ethic and she likes rice. Rice?

"How was your day, Greg? Did anything interesting happen? Did you eat any rice?"

"Did I eat any rice?" Whys is she asking me if I ate any rice?

I don't know what it is about Rose, but she has an addiction... well addiction might be to strong of a word. Let's call it an affinity with rice. She has rice for breakfast, lunch and dinner. She'll even have it as an afternoon and late night snack. I often wonder if she keeps some hidden in her purse so she can have a snack when she goes to work. I don't know what it is about rice, but I joke with her and tell her that she is **Powered By Rice**. And her response is, "Yes, I am powered by rice... and rice gives me energy to dance. Dancing is Life. Rice is Life!" I'm starting to think everything in the Philippines is *Life*.

Then Rose asks me a something on a different topic. It wasn't about my day, the weather or rice. But it was about my education.

"Where did you go to school? I want to know more about your life. You know, education gives you a chance to recognize opportunities. Opportunities give you a chance at a better life. A better life means you can eat more rice," she jokes.

So I explain to her that I graduated from The Ohio State University. "Some people would consider The Ohio State University as a city because the university has its own hospital, numerous buildings, student housing, an airport, shopping, restaurants, its own government, a police department, a fire department, and so much more."

"So if the university is that big, is it on a separate island?"

I have to smile at her innocent question. "No, it doesn't have its own island. The ocean is far away. The university is in the city where I grew up. Columbus, Ohio."

Which led to me asking Rose where she grew up.

"I grew up very close to where MacArthur returned during World War II. Have you heard of General MacArthur? He is a hero in the Philippines. My grandmother was a spy for him during the war. I grew up in Abuyog, Leyte. But not in a city. It's in the *province*."

The *province*? Hmmm, that's an interesting word. I don't know what a Filipino *province* is, and she can't find the words to explain to me. So I'm guessing from her description that a province is a rural area, or something similar to a very small town in the countryside. So I'm thinking along the lines of *Mayberry from the Andy Griffith Show*. She tells me she will show me where she grew up... (but that's another story).

... And she continues...

"I also want to graduate from college because I want to be a nurse," Rose tells me, "but I don't want to work in a hospital... or overseas. I want to work *for* the people of the Philippines. I mean I want to help those who cannot help themselves. You know... *the poor people*." She further explains, "When I was a child, my Grandfather was a doctor. This means I was a lucky child. If I got sick or hurt, then I got medical attention. But others in the *province* are not so lucky. They cannot afford or find doctors. So I want to help those people. The people who cannot afford doctors. I don't want to be a nurse for the purpose of making money. I want to be a nurse because I care for the Filipino people."

Her heart touching story is hart warming, but whats more amazing is her drive to achieve her goal, and how she is achieving it.

"The way I pay for school is by working 18 months in the sewing factory. Some of the money I send home to my parents, some I keep for rice, and some of the money I save the for tuition. When I have enough money saved for tuition, I go to school for 1 semester. Then I repeat. Like washing my hair. Wash - Rinse - Repeat."

In my mind I thought, "Hey, this is a respectable plan." But then I was surprised at the next thing she tells me.

"I know it's mindless work in the sewing factory, but it pays a good wage. If I were only taller, then I could make more money." (As I mentioned earlier - Rose is a petite 4 feet 8 inches tall — and in the Philippines, most jobs have a minimum height requirement of 5 feet 2 inches. Astonishing as it may sound, it's a ridiculous requirement for most jobs here in the Philippines).

"So what do you get paid each week?"

"We don't get paid by the week. We get paid by the month. For 9 hours a day, Monday through Saturday, I get a salary of $80 per month. That's if I make my quotas."

Eighty dollars a month! Oh my gosh. How can anyone survive on that. So without hesitating, I interrupt her, "Have you ever heard the scholarship they offer for nursing students who are no taller than 4 feet 8 inches?"

She looks me with sad eyes and pouts, "They don't have anything like that here in the Philippines. If they did, then I would apply."

"Well, there is one scholarship that is being offered, but unfortunately there is only one scholarship and it is being awarded today."

Instantly tears well up in her eyes, "And see, I missed the deadline to apply."

"Why are you so sad?" and I'm beginning to feel bad for teasing her this way. "Maybe you should be happy. Maybe today's *your* lucky day," I smile. "As a matter of fact, today *is* your lucky day because you've just been awarded the Great Things Come in Tiny Packages Nursing Scholarship... courtesy of me."

"Talaga? Talaga?! Really?! Really?!"

I nod, and her tears of sadness turn into tears of joy.

Jumping in the air, she throws her arms around my neck and kisses me full on the lips. "I will love you forever Greg Pasden."

"So you will love me long time?" I tease.

"I will love you long time. Forever. Whatever it takes to show you how much you mean to me."

"If you will love me more than rice, then I will be a happy man."

Needless to say this earns me a love bite.

Goodbye Condotel

I have to admit, living in a condotel has been — how should I say this — charming. The staff greets me as I enter the lobby, "Good afternoon Mr. Pasden". The restaurant has inexpensive tasty meals. The pool staff knows I like a pina colada when I get out of the pool. And I've even hired an affordable maid service for $1 per day. All this makes me feel spoiled, but sadly it's only temporary. The reason it's only temporary is because every 2 weeks I have to leave the Philippines to return to work. This means packing up all my belongings and taking them with me — there are no U-Store-It businesses here.

So why don't I just store my belongings with Rose? Or why don't I **move in** with Rose? I think she has the same idea.

"Greg, you can move into my apartment..."

This idea sounds good until...

"... I'm sure the others won't mind."

"What do you mean *The Others*?"

The Others - Well, Rose lives with her sister, her brother, her cousin and two friends. In the Philippines, this seemingly crowded mix is a normal and comfortable option. But to me, it's a claustrophobic event waiting to happen. I imagine it being like 20 sardines crammed into a 10 sardine can. So I politely tell Rose, "I don't want to impose on your family and friends," plus I have another proposal.

My proposal is to get my own apartment. What I *really* mean is to get an apartment with Rose - only Rose and not *the others*. I know she is very close to her family and friends, but I really hope she'll consider my suggestion over hers.

"Rose, can I ask you a question? You don't have to give me an immediate answer, but... What do you think about you and me getting our own apartment? I mean an apartment for just the 2 of us."

... And her eyes get *big*...

Her reaction is far from what I expected. Let me explain. Have you ever seen a super excited puppy. I mean like one that jumps up and down, and licks you because it's so happy to see you. Well, this is same the reaction I get — except without the licking.

She's jumping up and down, kissing me, laughing, and doing something else that resembles wagging her tail. When her energy level dwindles, she puts on a serious face, walks toe to toe with me. She jumps up one more time and wraps her hands around my neck pulling her face to mine... and with a smile she calmly says,

"If this is what **YO-O-OU** want, then I will be happy to find an apartment just for the 2 of us."

I nod my head in agreement and smile.

And it's the puppy dance all over again. "I am an excellent bargain hunter! And I will negotiate a good price. Very cheap. You'll see. Can I? Can I?"

And the decision is made. Rose and I will move in together. Unfortunately, I have to return to work again. What this means is that I will be away for at least two weeks, and I can't be here to help her decide on a place. So I put my full confidence in her bargain hunting and negotiating skills... because I've learned to trust Rose.

While I'm away, Rose is keeping me informed about the apartment hunting adventures. She's telling me "Oh, it was to cold," or "it was to hot," or "it was to big" or "to small". I'm beginning to think she is looking for apartments in the neighborhood where "Goldilocks and the Three Bears" live. But I know she is doing her best to find us a place to meet our needs. Plus the apartment hunting is making her happy.

Then one morning after a night of flying, I get a text message.

"Call me. I found our new home! Your cute girl who adores you, Rose".

I smile and login to Skype so I can give her a call.

If you are not familiar with Skype, then let me give you a quick explanation. It's a computer program that replaces your telephone (sort of)... but it's better. Instead of just hearing each others voice, now we can see each other face-to-face. It's just like talking to each other on TV (except through your computer). Rose and I like it because sometimes we cannot communicate with just words. Think Lucile Ball and Ricky Ricardo. Where I'm Lucy and she's Ricky. It's the language barrier thing. Many times she'll try to tell me something, but either the words don't come out right or she doesn't know the word for what she wants to say. So instead of her saying it, she'll often act it out in front of the computer screen, while I'll try to guess what she is trying to say. Rose is excellent at this, and it always makes me laugh.

The other good thing about Skype is being able to see each other. It makes it feel like we are almost together (even when we're separated by thousands of miles and 12 time zones). And with me traveling as often as I do, Skype allows us to look into each others eyes, whisper sweet nothings and be happy... even if we can't hold each others hands.

As soon as I login, she calls me. Then her jumping body appears on screen... "It's a great place! Very nice. Very cheap. You will be happy. It's so-o-o cute!"

Obviously she's happy and I can't help but share her enthusiasm.

"But..." then she gets shy and serious, "we don't have house supplies or *furnitures*. Can I buy some things? I want to make our new home nice for you."

These are things we need, so of course I agree.

"Don't worry. I'm a good shopper. You will like what I find. You will see. Call me tonight before you go to work and I will tell you what I bought for us. I will make you proud of me. Trust me." I fully trust she will do everything in her ability to find us what we need.

After we finish our conversation, I wire her what I think is enough money to buy what we need for our new place: one thousand dollars. Now it's nap time. I'll need to be rested before another night of flying.

A 4 hour nap feels like minutes, but my alarm clock tells me that it's time to get up and get ready for another night of flying boxes through Asia. I shower, shave, get dressed and I Skype Rose... and she is excited.

"Oh Hon, I found so many good bargains! And I opened a bank account for the money we had left over. You sent me much, much money? That's more money than people make in a year. Anyway, I hope you like what I buy. I buy us house cleaning and cooking supplies, new towels, and furniture. And a bed! A bed big enough for both of us to sleep in **at the same time!**"

"Big enough for us to sleep in *at the same time*?"

"Yes! This way we can share, and I don't have to sleep on the floor when you are sleeping on the bed."

I have to laugh because she is serious.

"Yes. In the other apartment with my sister, brother, cousin and friends... we didn't have a bed. We only sleep on the floor. But now we — you and me — we have a bed! A big bed!... And we can jump on it too! I tried it. It is very strong. You can do it too. Trust me."

I laugh more. Partly because of her innocent enthusiasm, and partly because I am amazed that Rose thinks sleeping on the floor is normal (well maybe it is for the Philippines, but not for me).

Sharing her enthusiasm, "Rose, I can't wait to be home and see what you've done."

Looking at the calendar, I realize it's only ten days before I get home in the Philippines. Each day Rose is giving me daily reports on the status of our new apartment... and there is a small problem. Rose says she can't sleep on our new bed. For some reason it makes her hot and sweaty. And the same thing happens when she sits on the new furniture.

I'm wondering, "Is she allergic to the furniture?" And Rose is asking "Will I be sleeping on the floor every night?".

Whatever the reason, I'm sure we'll figure it out together once I get home. But until then, Rose says she is staying off the furniture and sleeping on the floor.

Nine days later I land at the airport. I notice it's 5:30 in the morning as I walk out of the cargo terminal, and there's my Rose. Patiently waiting under a coconut tree, and putting an orchid in her hair. She looks up and sees me. "Mabuhay honey ko! Welcome home to paradise!" and runs over to give me a welcome home kiss. "Let's go! I want to show you *our* new home!" Seconds later we jump in a taxi, and off we go.

On the way she tells me the apartment is outside of Angeles City. It's an area called Dau (pronounced dah-Oo). She also tells me that she's washed the new furnitures several times but it's still making her sweat. She also imparts to me she'll be happy even if she has to keep sleeping on the floor. I hug her and silently let her know it will be alright.

Finally the taxi lets us out at our street. We pay the driver, Rose takes me by the hand and walks me to the door to our new home.

With a cautious smile, she unlocks the door and says, "I hope you like it?"

I smile. She did a remarkable job. She found us a delightful apartment and she made it an adorable home for two. The apartment is a small studio with pastel walls and tiled floors, and it has everything we need. Including the furniture... And immediately I know what's causing her sweating disorder... and I laugh.

"Rose, two things. First, I'm so happy and proud of you. You did an awesome job. And two, I'm pretty sure I know what's causing your sweating problem."

"You do? Can a doctor fix it? Do I need to take medicine?"

"No, I think I can solve your problem, but it will take a small amount of work on my part. Do you want to watch?"

"Of course I want to watch. I want to learn how you are going to heal me. I want to sleep in our bed with you."

As I walk over to our new bed, Rose tilts her head and looks at me apprehensively. I can see the gears in her head turning as she is wondering what I am going to do.

"Watch closely."

Bending over I put both hands on the mattress. But before I can do anything she says...

"Are you going to put a magic spell on the bed?"

I laugh again. "No, just watch."

Then I grab a handful of material on the mattress, and I pull. Then I pull some more and then it comes free.

Completely startling Rose, "What are you doing to our bed? Are you allowed to do that? Are you allowed to remove the plastic?"

I smile and nod my head.

"Really? Can you do that to the other furniture too? I didn't know I was allowed to remove the plastic."

After I stop laughing, Rose smiles and says, "Now that you've figured out what was wrong with the bed, what do you think about us testing it out together?"

"Do you mean jumping on it?"

"That's not the kind of test I'm thinking about. Guess again."

"I like the way you think."

Finding Transportation

Getting around in the Philippines is similar but a lot different from it is in the US. In the US, it seems like everyone has a car to get around, and most people don't use public transportation. In the Philippines it's the opposite. Public transportation is everywhere. I mean there is so much public transportation that it causes traffic jams because the streets are inundated with various modes of public transportation.

I'm sure you're familiar with a bus. In the Philippines, busses are only used for intercity transportation (for longer distances). I like riding in the busses because they are air conditioned, the seats recline, they play movies on an overhead TV, and they make regular stops where they pick up street food vendors to feed us a variety of foods.

In the city, instead of using a bus, the Filipinos have created something completely unique to the Philippines. It's called the Jeepney, and it's the Philippines most common form of mass public transportation. Thousands of them clog the streets of Manila, Cebu and Angeles City. From 6am to midnight, they will be jockeying for position on the main roads hoping to get the next 9 peso fare (9 peso is about US$0.20 or 20 cents). What's amazing is that they have no set pick-up or drop-off point, the streets are so crowed with these vehicles is that they are actually bumper to bumper and sometimes it is faster to walk than it is to ride in one. This chaotic low speed traffic congestion that reminds me of the traffic I would encounter right after a 4th of July fireworks celebration.

So what is a Jeepney? Jeepneys are made from the US military jeeps that were left behind from World War II and the Vietnam War... but with a unique artistic Filipino twist. Jeepneys look like someone took the old military hardtop jeeps and stretched them about 20 feet. Then the artistic Filipinos decorate their jeepneys with gaudy miscellaneous figurines, stickers and hand painted art work that men believe will make their cars go faster and attract more customers. I've seen some interesting artwork too. RedBull & Boeing stickers, wood carved Mercedes emblems, and bronco bull horns mounted on the grills. Apparently there is a plethora of stylized, junk yard artists tripping on San Miguel beer. I have to admit, some of these artists do some eye catching decorating, but they still haven't made a jeepney large enough for my 5 foot 10 inch frame to sit upright in. My head is always being crushed against the metal ceiling.

The other mode of public transportation is the "Trike". Trikes are motorcycles with sidecars that have roofs. They look fun and lots of the locals use them all the time, but guess how trikes are designed. They're built for the fun loving smaller people like Rose, but not for taller people like me. On one occasion Rose persuaded me to ride with her in a trike. Obviously it was fine for her, but for me it was like putting Lebron James in a Yugo.

So to make traveling around the city easier, Rose and I decided to buy the **most popular** form of transportation in the Philippines. Something practical. A small scooter. Something Rose can ride that is easy to ride, functional and economical.

"Hon, if we happen to see a cute pink scooter with a basket in the back, do you think we can get it? I think it will be very nice for us. What do you think?" Rose asks trying to contain her excitement.

"Pink? I don't really like the thought of pink. Maybe we can compromise. Red is a darker shade of pink. What do you think?"

She smiles, nods in concession and we walk inside the dealership.

Have you ever shopped for a new vehicle in a dealership before? Can you imagine what happens upon seeing raw power on 2 wheels, and hearing the thunderous sound of excitement? What do you think this does to a person? Apparently it can transform DNA and bring out the animal inside.

"Screw practical. We need Powerful and Sexy!"

And without even asking for the other's opinion, the following words came out, "Get us a red racing bike, 2 helmets and leather chaps for both of us."

And like an obedient salesman, he does just as he is told... by Rose. Yes, it is Rose who became overwhelmed with excitement upon seeing the racing bikes. It was like watching a little kitten transforming into this ferocious lioness (except an adorable tiny version).

And when her DNA returns to normal, the little brown eyed kitten looks at me and asks, "Can you teach me how to ride a motorcycle Hon? I don't know how to ride, but I want to ride. I'm ready to Ride Hon. Please! Please! Teach me! Teach me! I promise I'll do exactly what you say."

So instead of leaving the store with our practical pink scooter, we're riding away on sporty red motorcycle while wearing the newest safety gear — black leather jackets and matching chaps. I have to admit, Rose's new form fitting outfit radiates pure sexiness. She could easily pass for the fourth Charlie's Angel. And what do I look like?... Well how I look doesn't really matter...

"You look really cute Hon."

"Cute? Don't tell me I look cute. Cute's for kittens."

"Hehe!"

Friendly Police

Learning to ride a bicycle, a scooter, or a motorcycle requires plenty of space. So I have 2 places in mind: the cemetery, or the hospital. Realizing that someone might require immediate medical attention, I decide that learning to ride near the hospital is the more prudent choice.

After donning her leathers, her gloves and helmet, Rose climbs on the back of the bike, and off we ride to experience a new challenge.

The ride to the hospital takes about 30 minutes of driving through town. The streets are lined with many law enforcement officers, but I really question if they really know the laws — since I frequently see them driving on the wrong side of the street, without helmets, and letting people park in no parking zones. So it's not a surprise that we see a police officer on the side of the road as we ride to the hospital.

"Be careful Hon. It's the Police!"

"I will. Don't worry," and I pat her hands wrapped around my waist.

"He's staring at us!"

"It's because you look *hot* in your sexy black leathers," I tease.

Just then the police officer waves at us. That's friendly of him. I wave back as we ride by.

"Hon, what are you doing?!" Rose exclaims.

"I'm just waving back. I'm trying to be friendly. It's OK. See, he's waving more... but why is he running behind us?"

"He's not running. He's chasing us! He was telling you to pull over!" she excitedly explains.

"Oh well, we are well passed him now... but if he wants to continue chasing us down, **then** I'll pull over." This comment earns me a sharp pinch below the belt — apparently she isn't humored by my answer.

Minutes later I pull over... and just like I thought, the police officer is nowhere in sight.

"See Hon, the police officer stopped chasing us. I guess he realized we are going to the hospital," I joke — earning me another pinch.

As I get off the bike, she slides up front, and I ask, "Are you ready Hon? It's time for your riding lesson." Rose nods and smiles nervously. With a reassuring voice I encourage her, "Don't worry. You'll be fine. It's just like riding a bicycle."

"Really? That's good to know, but... but... I've never ridden a bicycle."

And without saying another word, she opens the throttle and off she goes. Slowly and carefully just like we talked about, except she's added something we didn't talk about. Lots of screaming. I'm not sure if her screams are for excitement or for horror. Nonetheless, can you imagine what happens when a woman is screaming in front of a hospital?

Seconds later the police, the doctors, the nurses, and the hospital staff come pouring out of the building like its a hospital fire drill, and everyone is looking for the screaming woman.

Knowing I need to act quickly...

"Don't worry, don't worry! Everything is OK. It's her first motorcycle lesson."

Immediately everyone goes from CODE BLUE mode to a hearty laugh. As soon as the laughter dies down, everyone does something that I never would have expected. Instead of going back inside the hospital, they all line the street to cheer and clap for Rose. They are encouraging her. They understand how she feels, because most of them have gone through this learning process too.

As the hours pass, the hospital staff slowly returns to their duties, until it's just me and the palm trees cheering for Rose. I signal that it's time to go home and Rose rides right up to me.

"I think I learned fast today because it's just like riding a 3 legged carabao. If you put you hands, legs and butt in the right place at the right time, then it doesn't wobble."

We both laugh, and makes me promise that we will do it again tomorrow.

On the way home we talk about what we both learned. Rose talked about how much fun it was learning the basics of riding a motorcycle, and I teased that her screaming in front of a hospital will get us a good humored audience.

All in all... it's another great day in paradise.

"Greg, do you see who I see in front of us?"

"Don't worry. I see him."

"You know what to do, right?"

"Of course I do...I know how to wave!"

VROOM!

"My Grandparents are Doctors"

Have you ever had one of those nights where you are laying in bed, and you can't fall asleep because your mind won't stop thinking? Well, this is one of those nights. And if you couldn't tell, I love being with Rose. I'm having many happy experiences with her, and now I'm thinking about asking her the all important question. I'm thinking to ask her to marry me. But I'm nervous and I'm wondering what she'll say. Will she say, 'Yes'? And if she says 'Yes', will we have a baby after we get married? If we have a baby, will our baby be a boy or a girl? What will we name the baby? When our baby grows up, will our baby be a doctor or a pilot? Will our baby will be athletic, creative, smart?... And all this nervous thinking has brought me to the point where I'm having a terrible headache.

So to quell the pain, I do what I've always done. I get out of bed and start looking for an aspirin... in our new apartment, in the dark of night, and I have no idea where Rose has put the aspirin.

Trying to be quiet while bumbling around in the dark for the elusive aspirin, I hear a sleepy voice ask, "What are you doing Honey? Is there anything I can do?"

"Sorry for waking you. I'm trying to find an aspirin for my headache."

"If you have a headache you should be waking me so I can help," she continues in her gentle voice.

"I'm a *big boy*. I can find an aspirin."

"Don't be silly. Let me take care of you the way I was taught to cure a headache," she gently insists. "Lay down on your back. I want to show you something."

"I like the way you're thinking," I tease.

"We're not doing *that*. Instead I want to show you something my grandparents taught me when I was a little girl. It really works. I promise."

"You have classes tomorrow. Don't you need your rest? I will just get some aspirin."

"Don't be afraid. We do this all the time in the *province*. My grandparents are **doctors**, and they taught me some of their techniques," she smiles and straddles my chest. "I'm going to massage your head," and she starts kneading my forehead with her little fingers. Minutes later my headache is gone. Just like she promised.

"Thank you Hon. That is much better than an aspirin."

"My pleasure," she smiles. "I knew it would work. Like I said, you don't need to take medicine when you have a headache because you have **me**. Just ask me to massage your head the next time you have a headache or body ache. It's how I show my love for you."

I smile.

"If I don't massage you, then you might get someone else to massage you. So if you don't ask me to massage you, then it means there must be other girls in your life."

"I'm not going to argue with your logic. I love your massages."

She smiles, "I'm glad I can make you happy."

"By the way, what kind of doctors are your grandparents? Chiropractors or General Practice? I need to thank them for teaching you that massage technique."

"You'll get your chance to thank my grandparents when we go tot he *province*. But they aren't chiropractors or general practice doctors."

"What kind of doctors are they?"

"They are Witch Doctors," she smiles and closes her eyes.

"Witch doctors? Are you kidding me?"

Rose sits up and looks at me. "Is your headache gone?"

I nod.

"Then stop worrying and go to sleep... or I'll turn you into a toad," she teases.

"Why a toad?"

"Have you ever seen a tongue on a toad?"

[NOTE from Rose: Why do they call it *Alternative Medicine* when it's the original medicine that humans have been using for thousands of years? Chemical medications were discovered about 100 years ago!]

Valentine's Day on Skype

Today is Valentine's Day. A traditional day for lovers to express their feelings through poetry, music, gifts and hopefully a little romance. Over the past year, it's become obvious that I've become close to Rose. Okay, more than close. I truly love Rose.

For the past few months I've been thinking of a special Valentine's Day surprise. My plan — make Rose breakfast in bed, convince her to play hooky from school, spend the day hiking the volcano, find a shady place for a picnic, tell her how much I adore her, and when the moment is right, get on my knee and ask her...

... Well, not so fast. Not on this Valentine's Day. Instead I'm waking up on the other side of the planet after another night of flying cargo.

And Rose... well she's attending another fun filled day of nursing classes in the Philippines. And as you can guess, this means that our romantic date isn't going to happen. Instead it's going to be something completely twenty-first century. We are having a Skype date where I can tell her... Well, you know.

It's seven o'clock and my computer starts chiming. Smiling I know Rose will have an interesting story to share. Why will she have an interesting story? Because I had a surprise delivered to her today. Not at home. But at her school while she was in class. And I'm looking forward to seeing what she has to say.

Clicking on my computer I instantly see Rose. She's smiling from ear to ear. In her hands are her favorite flowers. A bouquet of white and lavender orchids.

"Oh Hon, you're the best! Thank you so much for the beautiful orchids. You know they are my favorite. And all my classmates were teasing me, but I think it was because they were envious," she giggles. "And the poem is beautiful..."

"As I search the night sky above me,
A feeling captures my inner thoughts.
Thoughts that prove my longing for you.
For you are like night,
And without night I can never rest."

"Did you write that?"

"Yes, I wrote that poem."

"But I don't understand what you wrote below the poem... I don't know the language. What does it mean? All of my classmates and I tried to say it in class but we just sounded like robots saying Klaatu Barada Nikto. Here, let me try to read it to you."

"Nox et omnia mea te amo. Eripies me in sponsum vestrum? Numquid et vos eritis mihi in uxorem?"

"Oh that. It's a little something I wanted to say in the original language of romance - The language of the early Romans. It's a language called Latin."

"Latin? I don't know Latin? Can you translate for me?"

"Yes, I can translate it for you. Understand, my translation may not be completely accurate, and it's something that I wanted to say in person, but as you can see..."

"It's ok. You can say anything to me."

I smile. I get up from the computer and I take a few steps back. I get on my knee and I say, "You are my night and I love you completely. Will you take me as your husband? Will you be my wife?"

Immediately tears stream down her face. Rose tries to speak, but it comes out as squeaks. "Me? You really want to marry me?"

I smile and nod my head, "If you'll have me?"

... And I see her face **fill** the computer screen, and all I hear are sounds of sobbing.

"Are you ok? Is there something wrong?" I ask.

Then she backs away from the screen and I see her face filled with tears, "I'm kissing my future husband, and I'm crying. You've make me so happy. Of course I will be your wife. I am ready. You just tell me when."

"Will December fit into your schedule? It will give us time to invite friends and family."

... And I see her face and lips fill the computer screen again.

"Does this mean December is good?"

Can you help me get back to the airport?

Rose and I got married today at City Hall... along with 25 other couples. Not exactly romantic, but it is memorable because the mayor wanted Rose and I front and center for the proceedings. He told us having a foreigner getting married in city hall is an unusual event, and he wanted to have our picture with him for tomorrow's Christmas Eve news paper.

Unfortunately I won't be able to see tomorrow's news paper because tonight I need to return to work. Ugh! Can you imagine how you would feel if this happened on your wedding night? Fortunately Rose is understanding about the wedding night bad luck because she knows that while I'm working, I'll have an 84 hour layover on a resort island in Malaysia. Why would she be understanding about me staying on a resort island and missing our wedding night? Because she is going to fly to Malaysia so we can celebrate our honeymoon and Christmas together.

Now this trip will be Rose's first trip out of the Philippines. She's very excited, but she's very concerned too. First of all, she's never flown on a jet before, but this doesn't seem to bother her. I told her it's like riding a bus with wings — and she's ok with that. What she *is* worrying about is changing planes in Singapore before flying to Malaysia. This worries her because she has the fear of getting lost. Can you imagine getting lost in a foreign country and not knowing where to go to get help?

Even with her fear of getting lost in a foreign country, she is more excited about going on an exotic adventure to Malaysia.

On Christmas Eve, the flight to Singapore is empty, so it's like Rose has her own private jet with all the benefits — lots of attention from the friendly flight attendants, complimentary cocktails and any window seat she wants. Everything is going perfectly until...

"Ding! We will be experiencing turbulence from a thunderstorm. Please return to your seat, and fasten your seat belt. It's going to be a bumpy ride for the remainder of the flight."

"Miss Rose, we need to take away your drink and you must fasten your seat belt for the remainder of the flight."

"What's wrong?"

"It's just a safety precaution because we'll be..."

CRACK-BAM! Followed by horrendous turbulence. The lights go out... and then come on.

"Miss Rose I'm going to strap in next to you! This turbulence is..."

CRACK-BAM! And the interior lights twinkle like stars.

"This is the Captain speaking. Flight attendants, please prepare for landing and cross check."

The next words really spook Rose.

"Miss Rose, I'm not going to get out of the seat. I think it's to turbulent for me, so I will just stay here and pray all goes well before we..."

BAM!

"Miss Rose... I think we just landed. Let me check. Yes! Yes, we have landed! Let me help you out of your seat and you can exit the jet. We know you had your choice to fly with any carrier, but we really appreciate you flying with us today."

Quickly Rose unbuckles and runs off the jet. "Whew, that was **not** easy. Now I only need to find the other jet. I sure hope it's easy to find."

But when she gets off the jet, it's not what she expects. Instead of seeing a small, simple airport terminal, she finds herself in a massive, spectacular environment filled with glitzy lights, music and a plethora of stores — a Tiffany's boutique, a Porsche dealer, a Gucci store, and many other high fashion retail outlets.

"Oh my gosh, where am I? This can't be the airport? Did we crash at the mall?" and she begins to panic. "I am lost. What country am I in? I need to go to the airport," but the people around her ignore her delirious questions and usher her into the sea of shopping.

If you've never been inside the Singapore airport, then imagine a sensory overload with shopping and pampering. The Singapore airport is a high end retailers paradise with 5 star restaurants, luxurious hotels, cinemas, live shows and unimaginable spas. Any experienced traveler might think the same as Rose - 'I'm so-o-o-o lost'.

With panic creeping through her body and taking hold of her lungs, she quickly walks into the mass of people hoping to find someone to help her... but everyone ignores the confused little traveler. "Who should I ask for help? I don't know how to call for help. What do I do?"

Rose is not from the city or anything close to resembling a metropolitan area. Instead, she is from the remote jungles of Leyte. So to understand what it's like for Rose to be in this enormous facility filled with unfamiliar sights, lights, sounds and distractions, then think of a panicked rabbit being dropped into a crowded room — the cartoon *Ricochet Rabbit* comes to mind.

And just before Rose is about to run screaming through the airport, she sees someone she knows she can trust. An older gentleman. A Filipino maintenance man.

With tear filling her eyes she asks, "Excuse me Sir, can you help me? I'm lost, I'm afraid, and I don't know how to get back to the Singapore airport?"

The older gentleman laughs, "Young lady, you are in the airport."

"Really?" she sniffles.

"Yes, Miss. You are in the arrival terminal. But don't worry. If you are lost, I will help you." And like a father, he takes her by the hand. "Tell me where you need to go and I will take you there." Sobbing she tells him, and together he kindly escorts her toward her departure gate.

As they approach her gate she squeezes his hand tightly and looks into his eyes, "Thank you Sir. I'm so happy that you are here for me. I thought I was lost. I thought the pilot made a mistake and we landed at the mall. Thank you for being my angel," and she hugs him.

"It's my pleasure miss. Merry Christmas."

"Since It's Christmas Eve, Can I Wear the Red Dress my Sister Gave Me?"

When Rose arrives in Malaysia, it's obvious something is wrong. She is pale. She looks like the color of cream with a splash of coffee. Normally her skin tone is just the opposite — like coffee with a dash of cream.

As her passport is being returned to her she sees me, and she runs to me.

"Honey ko! Honey ko! Honey ko!" and she jumps into my arms. She is pumped full of adrenaline because the words coming out of her mouth are flying a mile a minute. "I was so afraid I would never see you again. We had many bumps. The flight attendant was afraid too. Then I thought our pilot got crazy and landed at a mall. Then an angel... I mean a man helped me when I was lost. He tells me I'm not lost. He helps me find the plane to you. I hug him. And here I am! Whew! Now I'm hungry. Do they have rice in Malaysia?"

A quick taxi ride and we arrive at the resort. I feed her a poolside lunch, and while she's eating she gets an *adrenaline crash* — her adventure on the flight and in the Singapore airport have exhausted her, and now it's all she can do to keep her face from falling into her food. I sign the bill, I take her in my arms to carry her to our room, and I put her to bed. Needless to say, she was asleep before her head hit the pillow.

I'm glad she's napping now, because tonight we are celebrating Christmas Eve with dinner and dancing. I learned from her family that a Filipino Christmas is a festive event. Lots of food, music, dancing and fireworks. But here on this island in Malaysia, I doubt think they'll be firing off any fireworks tonight.

I don't know if they even celebrate anything on December 25th.

After a well deserved nap and a shower, she prances out of the bathroom clad in a towel and asks, "Hon, since it's Christmas Eve, can I wear a red dress my sister gave me? She says it's to small for her, but it will probably fit me just right. What do you think?"

Tonight we were going to dinner in an elegant restaurant. So instead of wearing shorts and sandals like we normally do in the Philippines, we are both dressing up. I'm wearing slacks, and a nice black Tommy Bahama button down shirt, while Rose will be wearing her sister's red dress. I guess it's a hand-me-down, but I'm sure Rose will make it look nice.

"I think it will be fine."

"I hope the people in Penang are not offended by me wearing a red dress. I saw many women wearing colorful burkas in the airport and in our hotel lobby, but none of them were wearing red. Is the color red acceptable in Malaysia?"

"They reason the women are wearing burkas is because Malaysia is predominantly a Muslim country, but I think they are more progressive here. Maybe it's why they are wearing colorful and jeweled burkas... but I'm not sure why they weren't wearing red. Don't worry, the resort knows it's Christmas Eve, and I'm sure no one will be offended if you wear the color red."

"Hon, I also bought a Santa Claus hat to wear with my red dress. If I wear the hat, do you think people will stare at me?"

"If people stare, it will be because you look stunning... and I like the Santa hat idea. I think it will be a nice touch to compliment your red dress."

"I'm just about ready. I think a red dress is very festive. Christmas is festive, right? Can you take my picture?" she asks as I look into the dressing room.

"Oh my Gosh!" and my mouth drops open in amazement. Rose definitely made this red dress look good. Not only good, but sexy. Not just a little sexy. But 'Hot Rod' sexy.

Needless to say, this Christmas Eve in Malaysia, was done Filipino Style. Filled with laughter, dancing, singing, and making new friends. Rose and the band members became quick friends, and they even invited Rose on stage to sing where she rocked the club for the closing minutes of Christmas Eve. Then the countdown began.

"10-9-8-7..."

Rose looks at me with a serious expression, "Greg, I'm shy to tell you this, but I have to make a confession. Is that ok?"

I nod, tilt my head and wonder what she wants to confess.

"It's Christmas, and I have nothing to give you other than myself and my love. Are you ok with that?"

I smile, pick her up in my arms and kiss her long on the lips. "I couldn't ask for a more perfect gift. Because of you, I have never been happier. I'm happier than a billionaire."

"They live in the province..."

The Province? Where is this mystical place? Many Filipinos migrate to the cities to get jobs, but where do they migrate from? The Province. It's as if the province is some mythical land. Nevertheless, I'm intrigued.

"Rose, where is *the province*? You keep telling me you and your family are from the province, but where is the province?"

"Oh, you know. It's outside the city. Where rice and fruit grow. Lots of fresh air. People are nicer. Lots of joking around too. You will like it when I take you there."

"Now I understand." At least I think I do. "So the province is the rural area of the Philippines?"

"For some people, but not my people. My people are from the trees and the **bundok** (mountain)."

Now I am confused. The trees? The mountain? I'm sure her family doesn't live in trees. Maybe it means that they are similar to the American Appalachian people. So wanting to meet her parents, and grandparents, I ask Rose if we can go to the province to meet them on the weekend.

"Really!? You want to go to our province? I must warn you. It will be a long *journey*."

In my mind I'm thinking, "Who says *journey*?" Maybe if we have to go on a journey, then the province must be a mythical place.

"Sure, let's go. I can handle a *journey*. Bring it on. Bring on the goblins too."

"Don't say that," Rose says seriously. "The *dwendi* might hear you. They have very good hearing."

"I aint afraid of no ghost or goblins or *dwendi*. I hope we see one," I tease.

"Be careful what you wish for. It just might come true."

The weekend arrives and I'm ready for our short flight across the islands to meet her family (and hopefully some goblins). It doesn't take us long before we arrive on the island of Leyte to start our journey. Leyte is Rose's territory and she immediately goes into action. Minutes later she informs me that she's negotiated for our transportation. A 4x4 Land Rover with an experienced driver so he can drive us wherever Rose tells him to go. On the way we pass through small towns, then villages, then small villages, then the road ends... yet we continue driving. Now its obvious why we hired the 4x4 Land Rover with an experienced driver.

Suddenly the road gets worse. The driver becomes obviously nervous and begins rapidly complaining to Rose. Rose gets stern, jabbers back something, and points straight ahead. This unintelligible exchange continues while the road grows worse.

"Hon, is our driver concerned? Are you sure it's safe out here?"

"Don't worry," she confidently tells me, "I'm brave — unlike our driver. I'm familiar with what can happen in this area. I'll protect you."

I have to laugh. Partly to deflect my anxiety, and partly because I can't imagine a 4 foot 8 inches tall, little girl being this brave, or protecting me in the jungle.

"Are there any lions, spiders or snakes out here?"

... And before she can answer, we jolt to a stop.

"Stop na! Not good. I drive no more!"

Quickly our driver gets out of the vehicle, removes our bags and tosses them to the side of the

Land Rover. Enraged, Rose gets out of the car to argue with the driver. Confused, and against my better judgement, I get out and stand by her side. Seconds later the driver ushers us away from the back of his vehicle before he climbs in the 4x4 and locks the doors.

"Where are you going?"

...And he backs away until he's out of sight.

With a tinge of panic creeping up my spine, I ask Rose, "Hon, do you know where we are? Also, did you notice that the sun will be setting soon? What are we going to do when it gets dark?"

And in the calmest voice she smiles at me and says, "Oh, that's easy. We lay on the ground and go to sleep. Because it's dangerous to walk around here in the dark."

In my mind I'm thinking, "Go to sleep? Here? Is she crazy? How can I go to sleep after we've been abandoned... in the jungle! And I'm pretty sure there are wild animals out here that can eat us?"

Shaking my head, I try to think what we can do to improve our situation. But nothing comes to mind other than a line from *The Wizard of Oz*. So I whisper, "Lions, and Tigers and Bears. Oh my!"

"Don't say that. You'll upset the Dwendi," and it's becoming obvious the stress is affecting Rose too.

As the sun slips lower on the horizon, I try to relax so I can recall some of the skills from my survival training classes. But instead of thinking about survival training, I think about all the bugs that will be crawling on me if I fall asleep.

Sensing my anxiety, Rose hugs me and says, "Don't worry. We're together. What could possibly go wrong?"

As if on cue, there is a rustling in the jungle. It's coming from the tall grass just across the path. Moving to a safer position, we quickly put our luggage between us and the sounds in the jungle.

"RAHHHH!"

And 4 men run from the jungle, grab our bags, and dash back into the tall grass.

"What the Heck? They're stealing our bags!"

Suddenly Rose turns ferocious. "I won't let them get away!", and fearlessly she dashes off into the jungle.

"SHIT! SHIT! SHIT!" is all I can say. Immediately my 'Fight or Flight' mechanism kicks in and tells me to protect Rose. I charge into the jungle, but Rose runs like a rabbit and I'm just barely keeping her in sight as she pursues our bandits.

With the combination of the setting sun and the tall jungle grass, I can barely see Rose as the chase transitions from the tall grass to the deep, dark jungle.

"Run faster! They are slowing," she urges. "I'm catching up to them."

Ten steps later I'm stride for stride with Rose when she suddenly stops... And there's our luggage on the ground.

"Wow, I guess we got lucky. You must have scared them when you were catching up to them."

"Don't move! Don't say a word," Rose whispers.

Why did she say this? Then I look up from our luggage, and we are surrounded. It's no longer only 4 men. Now it's 10 bare chested, unfriendly looking men... and behind them, there are others. None of them are smiling, and everyone is holding a machete.

Then we hear some yelling.

"Siya ay may tuwid na ilong," yells the first man.

"Siya ay napaka- puti," yells another.

"Mukhang siya masarap sa akin," yells a high pitched voice.

"What are they saying?"

"They said you have a straight nose... you are very white and... are you look delicious."

I'm baffled. Do they want to eat us or what? Why do they notice my nose?

"What do they want?" I ask her.

Before she can answer an extremely muscular man approaches us. He must be the leader. He puts his hand in front of Rose's. He demands something while putting his hand on her head. Then he puts his hand on my head and before he can say anything...

"Are we your prisoners?"

He looks me in the eyes. He steps closer to where I can smell his breath and says, "You funny man."

Then he steps in front of Rose...

"Umaasa ako na siya ay may pakiramdam ng katatawanan. Sa tingin ninyo ang may gusto niya ang aming Joke? Maaari mong sabihin sa kanya mali-gayang pagdating sa pamilya."

Rose whispers, "Hon, he said for me to tell you something. Don't worry."

"Don't worry? I think they want to eat us!"

"The bad news is they want us to follow them to the village."

"What?!"

"Just wait... The good new is that they don't want to eat us because..."

"That's good! Because why?" I interrupt.

"Because this is tatay ko- my father." And her serious expression turns to a smile. "He hopes you like our family joke. Oh, and welcome to the tribe!"

Washed with relief, and pumped with adrenaline, all I can do is fall to the ground and laugh. I guess this was the right thing to do, because all the others joined in with their laughter.

Rolling on my back, I look up to Rose, "Hon, I really thought I was going to be 'white guy soup'."

"Be careful what you say. My gay cousin did say you look delicious."

Cape Cod?

Rose and her family are sharing stories about the village, enjoying being together again, and having a good laugh because I had fallen for their practical joke. I have to admit I was afraid, but in the end it was good fun.

Now it's time to continue through the jungle to their village to meet the rest of the tribe. This experience makes me feel like I've stepped back in time, because people are either carrying lit torches, wearing machetes on their hips, or riding water buffalo. Me? I'm just looking for spiders and snakes.

"How long will it take us to get to your village?"

"Not long. Just enjoy the sounds of the night. Soon we'll be at my parents' house. Then you can get some rest."

Earlier on the flight to Leyte Island, Rose was attempting to describe her parents' home to me. The only thing I really understood was " it's a pretty house made of wood." As you imagine, there is a *small* amount of confusion when Rose explains things to me. Sometimes she can't find the right words to say what she means. For example she'll say, "When I'm with you, your face can stop a clock," but what she was trying to say was "When I'm with you, time stands still." One version sounds romantic, while the other has plenty of room for interpretation. So when she's telling me that her family lives in *a pretty house made of wood*, I imagine a Thomas Kinkade painting of a beautiful Cape Cod house. Let's see what happens.

"Tatay, naayos mo ang tulay," Rose praises her father. "I'm telling Dad he did a good job fixing the bridge."

"Bridge? What bridge?"

"See it up ahead?"

I see something, but it's not like any bridge that *I've* ever seen. It's a single coconut tree laid across a ravine. It's narrow, and there's no side rails! So there's nothing to hold onto when crossing what looks like the Pit of Doom.

"Are you kidding me? You want me to cross this?"

Ignoring my obvious reluctancy to cross, Rose and her family cross the bridge as casually as if they were walking through the mall. Finally it's my turn. I look at the wobbly bridge and pause. In my mind I'm thinking, "Maybe I can just stay on this side of the river while she visits her family." I tell myself, "Tomorrow will be here soon enough. I can sleep with the creepy crawlies."

"Hon, it's getting darker. Are you coming? You're not afraid are you? Do you want me to hold your hand and help you across... like an old lady?" she jokes.

A few of her family members understand her and they are thoroughly enjoying her gentle teasing.

"Don't be a Rooster... I mean, don't be a Chicken. I know you can do it."

More giggling from the family.

Did you know that *fear* and *ridicule* are strong motivators. Motivators that can get you to do things you normally wouldn't do. Well, this is one of those ridiculing moments that's motivating me.

So trying not to look into the boiling water and rocks below, I tentatively placed one foot on the wobbly bridge to test it. "It seems sturdy enough," I try to convince myself. One by one, I place a foot in front of the other. "This isn't so bad."

"Great job, your half way here!"

... And for some reason I pause.

Now the river sounds louder, the bridge seems narrower, and my feet feel like cement blocks.

Realizing my breathing is becoming shallower, my vision is narrowing, I recognize that I'm beginning to panic. I start seeing stars. I blink my eyes. "Am I going to faint?"

"Look at me Hon!" Rose shouts, "Don't look at the bridge! Look at me! Focus on my voice!"

Looking across the ravine, Rose confidently stares into my eyes and passes me a reassuring smile. "Focus! Focus on my voice. You can do this."

With a few calming breaths, I blink my eyes, and I say to myself, "I can do this." It becomes my mantra. "I can do this. I can do this. I can do this!"

"Listen to my voice sweet hart," a warming voice tells me. "You're almost here."

One step becomes two, then three, and soon enough I'm across. Cheers erupt from the family, while Rose hugs me tightly. "See Honey ko, I knew you could do it... Now let's get going to the house. I'm hungry now Let's hurry! You don't want to be here with the spiders and snakes after the sunsets do you?"

As our march is ending and the sunset after glow paints the sky, I'm just able to catch a glimpse of the distant fire light from the village when Rose starts cheering, "We are here! We are here!"

Entering the village, I start looking around. I'm expecting to see the Thomas Kincaid Cape Cod house that I had envisioned. Looking around I finally find the beautiful little house... but it's quite different than I imagined.

Who remembers the TV series "Gilligan's Island"?

Do you remember the little village with the bamboo huts, palm leaf roofs, and hammocks for beds? Guess what? I'm now on the set of Gilligan's Island.

So when Rose was telling me about the pretty little house made of wood, well now I know what she really meant. Bamboo, no doors, no floors, and no windows... but it's the place she calls her "Home".

"Welcome to our Paradise!" she beams with pure happiness.

I look at her joyful eyes and realize that Paradise doesn't necessarily mean resort style living. Instead, paradise means being home. A home filled with a loving and caring family. It's also in a place where family, friendship, nature are blended together in a lush, tropical Eden. Realizing this, I look at Rose and say, "Yes it is Hon. Thank you for brining me to Paradise."

"I'm glad you like it," she smiles. "Now let's go catch some big spiders so we can play with them after dinner."

And as she runs off into the village to hunt for spiders, I yell to her, "Hon, you just ruined my perception of paradise."

"Hon, I need to go 'number two'. Where's the toilet?"

"What is Number two'?"

Urgently, I explain to her what I need to do, and she discreetly walks me into the high grass of the jungle. "You can 'number two' here Honey ko."

"You mean there is no toilet?"

Discreetly, she nods her head and whispers, "This is where we poo."

"What about toilet paper?"

"The banana leaves are the best. But if there are no banana leaves here, then you can use grass or a rock. Your choice."

Wouldn't you know... no banana trees in sight.

"Do you like Bar-B-Q? Tonight for dinner we are having Bar-B-Q'd *Peesh*"

Cooking over an open fire is what Filipinos call a Bar-B-Q.

"My parents are cooking *peesh* tonight. Will you eat Bar-B-Q *peesh*?"

"*Peesh*? What's *peesh*?"

"Peesh swim in the water. They have a tail. Like a shark."

"O-o-oh," I laugh. "I know what you mean. You mean *Fish*."

"That's what I said. *Peesh*."

"Sure, a peesh sounds good," I tease.

Being curious how our fish is going to be cooked, I decide to watch them prepare the food. I'm surprised when I see the size of the fish because they are very small. The longest one was probably four inches long.

"Rose, what kind of fish is that?"

"Delicious peesh."

Hmmm, that didn't really answer my question. So I asked her if they are sardines.

"I don't know what a sardine is. We just call them peesh."

Ok, I concede. I will settle for eating the unknown peesh that looks like a sardine.

When dinner is served, I'm offered the first choice of fish. I'm first because I'm the newest member of the tribe, and the guest of honor. Being like Goldilocks, I chose a fish that is not to big and not to small - I pick one that is just right. A three inch fish, and put it on my plate.

"Hon, they want to watch you eat it now so you tell them how you like it."

"What's the proper way to eat my fish?"

"Use your fingers and put it in your mouth."

Following her directions, I picked up the little fish and put the entire thing in my mouth.

"Oh no Hon, we don't eat the peesh like that. You don't eat the head and the tail. Take it out and just eat the middle."

Ok, I assume they don't want me to eat certain parts of the sardine. So I take a full bite of the middle of the fish, and begin chewing. "Crunch, crunch, crunch." Apparently, this sardine has plenty of bones inside.

"Hmmm," I wonder, "should I take the fish out of my mouth and pick out the bones, or should I just keep chewing so I don't offend the cooks?" So I choose the latter, and I keep chewing through the bones.

While I'm chewing, I'm getting curious looks from the family. And while I'm getting curious looks, I'm thinking, "How long do I have to keep chewing these fish bones before they are small enough to swallow." Needless to say I keep crunching away.

"Hon, why do you eat the peesh that way?"

Before answering, I thought it would be best if I swallowed the fish, bones and all. I swallow... Then gag. Oh crap, the bones got caught in my throat. Unable to answer Rose, I get on my hands and knees hoping to get the bones out of my throat.

While wondering if this Filipino fish is going to be my last supper, Rose ignores my gagging and asks me, "Hon, why do you eat the peesh that way? We use our hands to take the peesh off the bone before putting it in our mouth."

Gasping and choking on the bones, I realize *that's what Rose meant* when she told me, "***Use your fingers and put the peesh in your mouth***." Fish only — bones not included.

Realizing I'm choking, Rose's grandmother gets up, grabs a handful of freshly cooked rice and forcefully puts it in my mouth. She lifts up my head, she looks me in the eyes, and she says, "Swallow."

Remembering what Rose had told me about her grandmother earlier, I figured is best not to argue with a 'witch doctor'. I immediately comply, and - Hocus Pocus! No more choking, no more gasping for air, and I get off my hands and knees.

Rose looks at me and says, "OK, now that your done playing around, can you need to tell them how you like the peesh?"

Laughing and relieved, I tell her family, "Let me put it this way. I hope the bones come out easier than they went in."

Rose translates and laughter follows. Needless to say, that *was* my last piece of fish for the night.

After we finish eating, the men get up and start drinking coconut wine, the ladies and children helped clear the table, and that leaves three of us at the table — grandfather, the grandmother and me.

As they start to get up from the table, I rush over to the lady who saved my life.

"Salamat po, Lola." Meaning, "Thank you grandmother."

She then looks at me, and in perfect english says, "I need you alive. I want my first grandchild. To thank me, you must make me a grandchild tonight," and she gently pats me on the butt.

All three of us laugh. And then with a smile she says...

"I'm serious."

"Do you want to take a bath Hon?"

Last night, at the suggestion of Rose's grandmother, Rose's parents offered us the use of their bed. Happily we accept.

"Tell your parents thank you," and I smile and grandma.

The indulgence of sleeping on a soft, comfortable bed is going to feel great after a full day of cultural experiences. I can't wait to plop down in the bed.

"Here's our bed Hon," Rose smiles. "Do you like it?"

Hmmm, again it's another cultural surprise that I don't want experience.

"Where's the mattress Hon?"

"Mattress? We don't have a mattress. We just sleep on the bed."

The **bed?** Hmmm? Ok, let me try to explain this, because the bed does not look like any bed that I'm familiar with. Instead it looks like a spinal torture device created by people who promote business for chiropractors. Why do I say this? Because the bed is made of bamboo poles that are lashed together with vines.

"Hon, maybe I can just sleep on the ground."

Laughing and ignoring my suggestion, Rose knows what to do. Immediately she goes to other homes in the village to gather clothes from family and friends. Why is she doing this? Because Rose knows some cushion will be needed for tonight, and she knows better than to defy her grandma's instructions. I'm just happy her resourcefulness works. Can you imagine how painful *following a witch doctors orders* could be on a bamboo bed?

Then as the cock crows, I hear a sleepy voice. "It's time to get up Hon. You are dirty and smelly, and you need a bath."

I know what this means, and I'm a little shy on what's going to happen next. Bathing means we are going to the river.

Surprisingly and without hesitation, Rose walks to the river's edge, she undresses and she jumps in the water. Splashing, laughing and playing. "What are you waiting for Greg? Jump in! Don't tell me you're being shy?"

"Let me get something first."

Before we left home, I remembered Rose telling me that her family doesn't have soap at their house. Instead, they use something different. Something made from flowers, coconuts and palm oil. So being practical, I packed a bar of soap. Then what happened next is something that I never expected from a simple bar of soap.

"Hon, I have IVORY soap. Catch!"

While I'm tossing the soap to Rose in the river, everyone in the tribe takes notice.

"SOAP! SOAP!" someone shouts, and I'm shocked at what I see next.

From the village, everyone dashes to the river, they take off their clothes and jump in the water. They all want to bathe with the *white soap.*

Watching all these naked people in the water I sarcastically ask, "Rose, do you expect me to take off my clothes and jump in the water?"

"No Hon. Wait until later."

"Why?" I tease.

"Because they don't know you. You can't be naked in front of them yet. They don't know you enough to see you naked."

"Does this mean I can to wait until we get home before I can wash?"

"Yes, you better wait until later because you don't want to blind them with your white skin."

Apparently, them being naked in front of me is OK. But me being naked in front of them... well, that's a different story. Just like me being in the jungle is a different story. I'm like a peesh out of water. But my crash course in jungle life taught me many things. Like I learned how to gather food where I didn't think any existed. I learned how to make a fire with bamboo and a knife. I learned how to find water when there were no streams or rivers. I even found friendship with people I can barely communicate with. More importantly, I learned that I can be happy where ever I am — even the jungle of Eden - as long as I'm with Rose.

American Southern Style Cookin'

Our flight from the island of Leyte to Angeles City is less than 2 hours, and after several days in the jungle, my stomach is telling me it needs some comfort food. Food that is so familiar that it makes you feel happy and comfortable. I guess that's why they call it comfort food. So as soon as we land I take Rose for some good ol' American, Southern style cookin'.

My work friends told me about an American restaurant near the old Clark Air Force Base in Angeles City. "You got to get the *Red Beans and Rice*. It's delicious!" So after hearing my friends' raving review, I knew this was the place to go.

"What's the name of the restaurant we are going to tonight?"

"It's an American restaurant called *The Cottage Kitchen*. Have you heard of it? I hear they have good *Red Beans and Rice*."

"Do you mind if I have *peesh*? I love eating peesh and rice. I really want a pretty peesh for dinner."

Teasing her I reply, "Sure Hon. You can have a pretty fish for dinner." And I try to imagine what a pretty fish looks like.

Entering the Cottage Kitchen restaurant, we immediately learn that my friend's review was spot on. The atmosphere and the uniforms immediately made me think I was in an authentic Southern home.

I order the red beans and rice, and Rose orders fish. The hospitality, the service are first rate, and the food is delicious... including Rose's pretty peesh.

After dinner, our Filipina waitress asks, "Sir, would you or madame like to try one of our signature deserts?"

I look at Rose. She smiles and nods yes, "I'm willing to eat almost anything."

"Do you have any House Specialties that you can recommend?" I ask.

"Yes, we do Sir. We have a Peach Cobbler made with a real Georgia Peaches."

"You really have Georgia Peach Cobbler?"

"Yes, Sir."

"Is it hot?"

"Yes, Sir. It is hot."

"Does it come with ice cream?"

"Yes, Sir. Vanilla ice cream."

"I'm going to get one," and I look across and Rose and ask, "Do you want to try one of your own Hon?"

And with a confused look on Rose's face, she sticks her tongue out as if to say, "Yuck" and says, "I've changed my mind. I don't think I want any desert."

I nod to our waitress and she dashes off to fetch me my hot peach cobbler with vanilla ice cream.

Unbeknown to me, Rose has never heard of term *cobbler*, and she doesn't know there is a fruit called a *peach*. Therefore, she has no idea what to expect before my peach cobbler arrives. So with curiosity she asks, "Hon, is this desert salty or sweet?"

"It's sweet."

I can see in her face she wants to ask another question.

"Does it have chocolate syrup on it to make it sweet?"

"No Hon. I think they make it with sugar to make it taste sweet."

Then she asks, "Is it soft?"

"Well, if it's cooked right, then the outside will be crispy and the inside will be soft."

With more confusion on her face, she asks, "Do you think mixing it with ice cream is a good idea?"

"Oh yes. The ice cream melts on top and gives it a delicious creamy texture."

Still confused she continues her questioning, "What shape is it?"

And before I can answer my Peach Cobbler arrives at the table. And it's served in a bowl and topped with a scoop of vanilla ice cream.

Rose asks another confusing question, "Why is it square and not shaped like a little person?"

I have no idea why she's asking such a silly question so I offer her the first bite. "Do you want the first bite Hon?"

Vigorously she shakes her head 'No', and she watches me smile as I put a spoonful in my mouth.

"Mmmm, this is excellent! You don't know what you're missing. Are you sure you don't want to have a taste?"

With a sour expression on her face, "How strong is the **peesh** taste?"

Nearly spitting out my mouthful, I cough, "*What?*"

"It's a *Peesh Goblin* right? Does it taste like peesh? I don't understand why it's square and not shaped like a little goblin or a little peesh."

I burst into laughter realizing Rose's confusion. She's thinking the waitress is not serving me Peach Cobbler. Instead, she thought I was being served a Fish Goblin.

Communication is a funny thing. Fortunately Rose can speak more english than I can speak tagalog. Maybe I should learn how to speak tagalog.

Obviously, I Don't know What I'm Saying

"Hon, I'm going to shower before dinner because *malibog ako*. Am I saying that right?"

I think it's a good idea for me to learn the local language since I'm living in the Philippines. It seems like the right thing to do. So I have been practicing with a few phrases that Rose has been teaching me. Rose gets a laugh because she thinks I talk like a baby.

"It depends on what you have in mind."

"I'm trying to say *I'm smelly*."

"Oh really! What you said does not mean *I'm smelly*. Instead you said *I'm Horny*. Smelly is *Mabaho*. So you should say *Mabaho ako* or *I'm smelly*."

"Do you like *malibog ako* better?" I ask.

"I think you better take a *cold* shower. But before you get in the shower I wanted to know if you want anything special from the market. I'm going shopping *bukas ng umaga* (tomorrow morning)"

"I think I'll go along with you. I need to get a haircut at the mall."

"I said I'm going to the market, not the mall. You can join me, but I know **you** don't like the market."

Rose taught me that the farmers market is the best place to get the freshest selection of meats, fruit and vegetables. As I mentioned before, Rose is a bargain hunter. She enjoys looking through the variety of foods — touching them, smelling them and finding the best foods for us.

"You are welcome to join me, but don't let people see us together, or you know what will happen... We'll get *Foreigner Pricing*."

Foreigner Pricing is code for the price will double.

"Saving money sounds good to me, so I'll steer clear of the market. But do you know if there is a barber nearby so I can get my hair cut?"

"There will be plenty of people chopping things with knives. Maybe we'll find someone with scissors. If not, I'm sure someone can chop... I mean cut your hair," she teases.

I laugh and jump in the shower wondering if she's serious. Nevertheless I'm willing to go have a look around the market. Who knows, I might find a really good barber.

Early the next morning, I go jogging. I like jogging in the morning because it's cooler and I can enjoy watching the sun rise behind our local volcano. It's a dormant volcano, but it's still a volcano and a beautiful sight to see.

When I first started jogging in Dau, I thought it strange that it strange living near a volcano. But not as strange as where I go jogging.

Where I jog there's no traffic, the air is fresh, and I hear the sounds of nature. It's peaceful, my jogging doesn't bother the residents, and the residents don't bother me... because the place where I jog is the cemetery.

Jogging in a cemetery might seem like a strange place to jog, but Angeles City doesn't really have any other places to jog. So when I saw the cemetery, I asked, "Why not?" And since no one answered me, jogging here has become part of my morning routine. But if the residents ever do say something, then I can guarantee that I will never jog in the cemetery again.

Thirty minutes of jogging and I return home to hear, "Oh! Honey ko, we need to go **now**. Early shoppers get the freshest and best food from the market. Hurry, hurry! Early birds eat better worms."

"Do I have enough time to shower first? *Mabaho ako*." Or is it *malibog ako*?

"No shower. No time! We need to go now. **You** don't need to impress anyone. Only impress **me**. And you're sexy in my eyes. So let's go *mabaho* man. Hurry, hurry. I want to buy you the best food... to make me sexy for you." She smiles... and off we go.

I do not, by inclination or by temperament, gravitate to places like an open market. I am intimidated and made uncomfortable by disorderly places where everything doesn't work smoothly, but where the people seem oddly content. But here I am today outside an open market with my loving and frugal wife who is intent on finding me a delicious bargain under the guise that it will make her sexy.

As we drive into the parking area, it's easy to see that the market is not a place for men because this place is filled with ladies. Only ladies. Ladies of all ages. Gossiping and arguing. Shopping and bargaining. Pushing and laughing. It's kind of reminds me of the mania one would experience shopping for gifts on Christmas Eve, but with the extra fragrance of freshly cut meat.

Yes, everything is fresh. Eggs, mangos, bananas, rice (of course, we must have rice), and the freshly prepared fish and livestock. Oh, the pungent fragrance of freshly cut meat makes my nostrils long for something more suitable. Like the rich aroma of a cup of steaming, brewed java. Unfortunately there are no coffee barristers to be seen. Instead, I will be enjoying a refreshing **buko** juice (juice straight from the coconut).

"Greg, why don't you go to that hair salon across the street? I use it all the time. Maybe you can practice speaking Tagalog."

"Hon, that's a ladies salon. It's *not* a barber shop."

"Don't worry. I see men in there all the time. They get their hair cut by the lovely ladies. Go have a look."

"You won't get jealous if a lovely lady is running her fingers through my thick, dark hair?"

"I have nothing to worry about," she smiles. "I'll see you when I'm done shopping. I can't wait to see what they do with you," and she rushes off into the pandemonium of marketeers. All to find us something nutritious, delicious and fresh, while saving a few pesos.

As I walk through the doors I quickly realize this salon is like not like any barber shop I've been in before. One - it's a salon. And two — all the ladies are wearing short mini skirts, tight tops, and high heels.

And as the doors close behind me, I hear, "Welcome *Sir*. How may *we* help *you*?"

"I know this is a salon... Um... but can I get a haircut? My *wife* says it's okay, and um.... she said other men get their haircut when she's in here."

"Oh, *Sir*. We can do that... and much, much more for someone as handsome as you. And we'll be happy to take good care of you."

Feeling a little nervous, I try speaking some tagalog. I'm hoping it will help me relax.

"Ok, I would like a haircut to make me 'pogi' (handsome). Oh and I have to warn you. I went jogging earlier today, and I haven't showered. So I am *malibog*."

"Oh *Sir*!" she and all the other ladies giggle. "Thank you for informing us that you are *'malibog'*. You speak Tagalog very well! Since this is your first time here, would you prefer someone tall or short to cut your hair? We have many ladies to choose from."

"I don't have any special preference. I just want someone who can give me a good hair cut so I will be pogi for my wife."

Notice I keep stressing that I have a wife.

As if on cue, a tall blonde walks out from behind a curtain. She's wearing a tight black velvet halter top, a very short mini skirt and thigh high boots.

"Hello Sir. My name is Erica. It will be my pleasure to service you. Would you like a *normal* service? Or do you have something else in mind?"

My jaw falls open and for a moment, words escape me... So before I can answer, Erica takes me by the hand and leads me to her salon chair.

As we walk to her chair her high heeled boots click on the polished tile floor, while my mind screams, "What did my wife send me into?"

"Hi Erica. My name is Greg. Um, I'm new to this. What's *normal* service?"

"It's a haircut with a few extra services. You'll love it. All the men do. Don't worry. It's nothing *naughty*" she giggles. Then, with a wink, she calls out, "Toni, Charlene. Please come and join us. Sir Greg would like the normal services."

As 2 tall, ladies clad in sexy outfits join us, my mind screams, "What did Rose - my wife — get me into?"

Forty-five minutes later, Rose is finishing up her shopping. She puts the groceries in the car, crosses the street, enters the salon, and sees me in the salon chair with my hands being massaged by Charlene, my feet being massaged by Toni, and Erica cutting my hair. Immediately Rose does something that shocks me. She smiles. Not just a simple smile. But she smiles like a Cheshire cat. She appears to be getting a huge thrill out of watching me get pampered by 3 tall and seductive ladies.

"Kumusta ka Ms Rose. Asawa mo dito na... and he says he is 'malibog' because he went jogging today" and the salon erupts in laughter. "Is this normal for him?"

Rose is laughing too. "I can see he's practicing his Tagalog."

"Yes, he is so cute," giggles Charelene. "We are teaching him a few things too."

A few minutes later, Rose pays the cashier for my haircut, she tips the ladies, and we cross the street to our car. She doesn't look at me, but she asks "Do you like your haircut?"

"The haircut is nice. Um... was it expensive?"

"No, it's the same price as your regular barber shop." And I notice while she's asking me these questions, her voice sounds odd. Then she asks, "Did you like the service they gave you?"

"It was Great! I can't believe they pampered me so much. Sooooo... you're not jealous?"

"Jealous? Me? No. Not at all," and she starts giggling.

"I've got to tell my friends in the States about this. They won't believe that I got this kind of service with a haircut."

"Are you sure you want to tell them?"

"Of course. Why not?"

"Because Charlene, Toni and Erica are 'Bakla'?"

"Bakla? What's a Bakla?"

"Bakla are not normal ladies."

"Does Bakla mean sexy ladies?" I ask.

Laughing harder, Rose answers, "No Hon. Bakla means lady-boy... and by the way. You didn't tell them you were 'smelly'."

Valentines Surprise

Do you like being romantic? I don't know if it's romantic, but I enjoy making Rose breakfast in bed, giving her flowers, and taking long evening walks. Well, this February will be our first Valentine's Day together, because last year we had to spend it on Skype. But this year I'm home so I want to do something special.

With the sun beginning to shine through the window, I lean over and kiss Rose. "Good Morning Sunshine! I have special day planned with fun and surprises."

"That's great Hon," she grins sleepily. "I have a special Valentine's surprise for you too... but it can wait until later. Speaking of later, would you mind if we sleep a little while longer? I'm very tired."

"Sure Hon, enjoy your beauty sleep. While you sleep I'll prepare your first surprise," I smile knowing this gives me more time to enhance her breakfast — hehe.

Here in the Philippines, flowers seem to grow everywhere, and Rose loves flowers. So before marking her breakfast, I spend time collecting some fragrant flowers while chatting with our neighbors. While the ladies seem envious, their men are signaling me to be quiet. Nevertheless, I now have fresh picked flowers to go along with her tropical fruit, and hot coffee.

Entering our bedroom to deliver Rose her breakfast I hear, "I didn't know my husband was sending me a sexy waiter to serve me breakfast in bed," she smiles seductively. "Is there anything else he wants you to give me in bed?" We both laugh and enjoy our breakfast.

After breakfast we get dressed and drive 3 hours to Subic Bay. Subic Bay was once a beautiful American Naval base, but in 1990, the lease was not renewed, and the locals turned many of the building into office and hotels with private beaches. Today we are enjoying 1 of them.

While plashing in the surf, drinking juice from coconuts, and enjoying the sunshine I see some people flying beach kites.

Pointing them out to Rose I ask, "Have you ever flown a kite?"

She looks at me and her eyes get really big, "Do you think I could do that? They look so big!" She looks back at the colorful kites dancing in the sky and says, "It looks so exciting! I'll do it if you hold me."

Soon we are flying a colorful kite. Zipping left and right, up and down, and laughing as we get pulled through the sand. The kite is more powerful than we expected, so Rose's idea for me to hold her was a smart idea. Otherwise she'd be flying up with the other kites.

Thirty minutes later we return the kite to the kite shop, and we head over to the Ocean Adventure Park for a personal encounter with a dolphin and a whale. What's a personal encounter? This means we get in the water, swim and interact with them.

Clearly concerned Rose says, "You know I don't know how to swim. What am I going to do if the water is over my head? Who will rescue me?"

"The dolphin and whale trainer will be with us and I'm sure they know how to swim. Plus I'll inform them you can't swim and I'm sure we'll be wearing life jackets before we even get close to the water."

"Thank you Hon. That makes me feel better. Otherwise I would be to afraid to do this."

Showing our tickets, we're escorted to another private beach where we'll do the encounter. As we approach the bay, a lady is riding the dolphin and the man is riding the whale and it looks like they are about to finish *their* personal encounter.

Laughing as they get out of the water, they turn and clap to show their appreciation.

"Hon this looks so exciting!"

As the trainer is helping the lady and the man get out of their life jackets, I decide to walk over to ask them about their adventure... But not Rose. Instead...

... She walks into the water and examines the dorsal fin of the whale. Then she gently pets and talks to the whale. Next she does something unfathomable. She climbs on the back of the whale! Immediately the whale goes into its routine and swims into the bay with Rose screaming!

"Help! Help me!"

At once I run into the water and try to swim after them, but I'm no match for the larger whale's speed and ability. While I'm trying to swim, the trainer mounts the dolphin and together they zip past me on a rescue mission.

And the **screaming** continues! But it's not what anyone expects. "Hon, this is GREAT! Can we keep him?!"

At that moment the trainer and the dolphin join Rose and the whale. All 4 of them return to shore just like the previous couple. Dismounting, Rose kisses the whale, and waves at me as I'm swimming to shore. "That was fun! What's next?"

Getting out of the water I'm getting ready to ask why she did that, but before I can get the words out she says, "That was fun! I wasn't afraid because I was riding on a dolphin. Dolphins rescue people, right?"

"Yes Hon, dolphins rescue people. But I have something to tell you. You weren't riding a *dolphin.* You were riding a whale!"

"Really? It sure looked like a dolphin to me," and we both laugh.

After our *structured* dolphin and whale encounter, our Valentine's Day date continues, but at a more subdued level. We tour the Ocean Adventure aquariums, enjoy shows, and we even do a little shopping where Rose decides to buy the whale. Not a real whale. A stuffed toy whale. Something to remind us of our adventure.

As the sun approaches slides lower on the horizon, our bellies remind us that eating is required event too. Eyeing a tiki themed restaurant Rose asks, "Do you think they serve pretty peesh?" I nod while hoping they serve my favorite — potent pina coladas.

Our native themed waiters and waitresses seat us in a bamboo bungalow close to the water. The sound of the waves, the sand under our feet, and the smell of the freshly cut orchids create a magical setting for us to enjoy our sunset dinner.

Staying in the native theme, our fish is served on platters made of banana stalks and leaves, and our pina coladas served in real coconuts.

The food is colorful, flavorful and delicious. This setting would make a great picture for Facebook, but Instead of interrupting the moment with a selfie, we just enjoy being together.

"Rose, do you remember what happened this time last year?"

"I do, and" ...her face looks like she's just seen a ghost. "Now it's time for your surprise Hon." And with urgency she say, "Do you have our plastic bag with the toy whale inside?"

I hand her the bag with her little stuffed whale inside, and I wonder what is so urgent.

Now she is trying to get the toy whale out, but the whale is to big to easily pull out. Instead she does something that really confuses me. She shoves her face into the bag... and vomits.

With an embarrassed look on her face Rose looks into my eyes and says, "That's not the way I wanted to do this, but that's your surprise."

"Wow Hon. That's so nice. Just what I've always wanted. A vomit covered stuffed whale?"

"No silly. Not the whale," she smiles. "We're having a baby."

We hug, we laugh, and I make her take a drink of water before I kiss her. It's the perfect Valentine's Day gift. We couldn't be happier.

... And if you are curious... Yes, we still have the little stuffed whale.

Pregnancy and :-)

Rose's gynecologist is great and her pregnancy is going normal. The baby doctor says to expect the baby on October 22. The timing is perfect because I started my vacation 2 days ago, Rose will be finishing her nursing exams tonight, and her mother will be here on the 20th. Believe it or not, I am really glad her mother is coming to help, because I don't have a clue what to do with a baby, or my wife after the delivery. My mother-in-law should have plenty of experience because she's given birth to 10 babies — in the jungle. So helping my wife, even in our twenty-first century cozy apartment should be a cinch for her.

Rose's final nursing exam will be finished by 7pm and I know she'll be exhausted. That's why I got here 10 minutes ago so I can pick her up as soon as she comes out of the building. I've also brought 2 of her favorite foods as a surprise to celebrate. Green mango with chili salt, and spaghetti.

At the stroke of 7 o'clock her classmates slowly flow out of the building looking like hungry zombies. Not for brains, but for the food I'm holding for Rose.

"Kuya Greg, you are so nice. Rose is so lucky to have someone surprise her like you."

Rose loves surprises. As a kid, she never had surprises. As you can imagine, growing up in the jungle is a hard life. No one really thinks to be romantic or creating surprising moments in the jungle. Instead it's more like survival of the fittest. So whenever I give Rose a surprise, she genuinely appreciates it and gets very happy. Happy like she's just opened a box of cute, baby puppies.

Speaking of baby, why hasn't Rose come out of the building yet? I look at my watch. It's 7:13 p.m.! I look back at the building and I see one last person is walking down the hall, and it's not Rose. It's her teacher. Something's not right.

Beep! Beep! A car pulls up next to me and rolls down the dark window. It's Rose's classmate. Half panicked I ask, "Have you seen Rose? I can't find her."

"Don't worry kuya Greg. She's in the backseat of my car."

"Is she giving birth?!"

"I hope not," she teases. "We finished our exam early so we came out here to listen to music and snack while waiting for you. I think she's asleep."

"I'm not asleep. I'm just checking my eyelids for cracks," she jokes. "If you are ready Daddy, can you take me home? My brain is exhausted."

Relieved knowing that Rose and our baby are well, I thank her friend while I help Rose into our car.

Rose loves her mango and spaghetti surprise and she eats quickly as we pull out of the parking lot. Even though the drive home takes only 5 minutes, I think the stress from Rose's nursing exams, the fatigue from carrying the baby and the spaghetti overdose are causing her to fall into a food coma. Putting the car in park I lean over to give Rose a kiss, but then I have second thoughts. She has fallen asleep with uneaten spaghetti still hanging from her mouth.

So instead of a kiss, I unbuckle her seatbelt, take her in my arms and I carry her inside. As I'm carrying her, she wakes up and kisses me with her spaghetti lips as I lay her in a pile of pillows. Why a pile of pillows? Because one night she *reluctantly* told me that laying on her back was so uncomfortable that she couldn't sleep at night. (The reason I say *reluctantly* is because it's not in Rose's nature to complain about anything. So when she told me that she was uncomfortable, then I knew it meant that it was *ex-*

tremely difficult for her). To solve the discomfort, I bought a dozen or so pillows. I positioned them so she could find a perfect position to be comfortable. The pillow position must be perfect tonight because she's doing something else very unnatural for her. She's snoring... And thankfully she is snoring, because I know she's getting the rest she'll need for the upcoming delivery.

Snoring - how do I deal with it? Honestly I'd prefer not to hear it, but it's a minor thing that I can deal with effectively. I'm using ear plugs, and tonight I'm pushing them deep into my ears so I can avoid the dulcet, nasal symphony - I'm getting sleepy too.

(Hours later...)

... "Ouch!" and I'm awake. "I hope that wasn't a lizard biting me."

"I'm sorry Hon, I was trying to gently wake you, but a gentle nudge didn't seem to work. So I thought a little 'Love' pinch would wake you."

I turn on the light and look at her. The pain in her face is obvious.

"Are you in pain?"

"Does a monkey like a banana?" she winces. "I think it's time we go to the hospital."

Minutes later we arrive at the hospital, and Rose's doctor is already there with another mother in labor.

"Bring her in here. She can join the party. We'll deliver two babies at the same time. It's not a problem. I'll even give you a discount," her doctor jokes.

An hour passes and it seems like the other lady and Rose are having a competition to see who can deliver first. While the other lady is screaming with each contraction, Rose only whispers. "Ouch!"

Another 4 hour pass and the competition ends. Rose's labor continues while the other lady celebrates the birth of her fifth son.

"Hon, this pain is terrible. Would it be OK if I cuss?"

"Rose, you can do whatever makes you feel better."

The doctor re-examines Rose. "Mrs Pasden, your baby is very big. You're going to need a C-section."

Rose and I had discussed this at length and she really didn't want to do a c-section. Not because she is against having the procedure, but because she doesn't want an ugly scar.

"Doctor, can you assure Rose that you will make her a pretty scar below the bikini line?" I joke.

"Don't worry. This week's special is a cute 'Smiley Face' scar. You'll love it down there."

Rose agrees to the procedure. The papers are signed, I'm scrubbed and gowned (so I can watch) and the procedure begins... and ends before I know it. We have a daughter.

"Doc, don't forget," I remind her with a smile. "Rose wants a pretty scar."

"I'll make it pretty. Come and watch."

As I watch, the doctor stitches Rose up, she takes out her Sharpie marker, and she adds two eyes. "See, I told you I'd make her a cute 'Smiley Face' scar. Now let's go pierce your daughter's ears. I'm giving her two gold hearts. My treat!"

As they roll Rose into recovery, the doctor pierces our daughter's ears.

"What are you going to name her?" one of the nurses asks.

"My father always said he loved April in Paris. So we'll name our daughter Aprilynn Paris."

"Excuse me Mr Pasden," interrupts the doctor. "I have some good news and I have some bad news. The good news is that Rose and your daughter are perfectly healthy, but they will need to stay here for a few days . The bad news is that the hospital is full. So she will have to either share a room with 2 others, or there is the expensive VIP suite. What do you want to do?"

Not knowing how much any of this is going to cost I have to ask, "What's the price for the VIP suite?"

"One Thousand Pesos," she replies sheepishly.

"Really? One thousand Pesos? Are you serious?" I ask in disbelief.

"Yes, Sir. I know it is expensive, but it includes a bed for your wife, you and complimentary breakfast and dinner."

I then think to ask, "What will be the *total* price for delivery and the suite?"

"I'm sorry Sir. It was a very expensive procedure. There is my doctor fee, the anesthesiologist's fee, the operating room fee, the 5 nurses, and the nursery. All-in-all it will be almost sixty-thousand."

In shock I ask, "Pesos?!"

"Yes, Sir. But don't worry. We can give you a 5% discount if you pay *cash*."

A huge grin grows on my face because I am completely amazed at how affordable health care is here in the Philippines. Sixty-thousand pesos is equivalent to US$1,500. Almost 20 times less than what we would have paid for the same procedure in the States.

"Doc let's give my girls the royal treatment. Put them in the VIP suite, and order us a bottle of champagne."

"I'm sorry sir, but we don't have champagne," she says seriously. "We only have rum and beer. Will that be ok?"

"Sure!" I choke out in disbelief because I can't believe the hospital actually serves alcohol. Maybe it's because the alcohol kills the germs. Whatever the reason is, I'm not going to complain. I'm going to celebrate! My two girls are healthy, and I'm a happy dad in paradise.

Don't worry - Do you know what that means?

"Mr. Pasden, now that you're new daddy, we need you to complete some paper work. It's for your daughter's birth certificate. Can you come with me?"

Rose is napping, so I follow the nurse down the hall to an office.

"Here you are Mr Pasden. Can you complete these forms. It should only take a few minutes. Our secretary will type up your daughter's birth certificate after you have completed the forms. If there is anything you need, just let me know and I will personally see to it."

Completing the forms are easy. Everything is in english and all I have to do is add our daughter's new name and other pertinent information about Rose and me. Like our address, dates of birth, nationality, and so on. But the next form is a blank birth certificate. Nothing on the form is filled in. So I find the nurse to ask her, "Excuse me miss. Did you know that you gave me a blank birth certificate?"

"Yes, Mr Pasden. Our secretary will complete the form later. We just need you to sign your name and your wife's name at the bottom."

"But it's a blank document."

"Yes, I know."

"What if the secretary makes a mistake? What if she puts down she's a *boy*, or misspells her name? I don't think it's a good idea to sign a blank birth certificate."

"Oh Mr Pasden, don't worry. This is a *hospital*. We are *professionals* here. This is the way we do things in the Philippines. We do this all the time. If there is a problem, then it can always be changed. Don't worry."

Have you ever seen the cartoon where there is an angel and a devil sitting on each shoulder? This is exactly how I'm feeling. One is telling me, "Don't sign it" while the other is saying, "You should be more trusting. She said they are professionals, so just sign it. What could possibly go wrong?"

I'm not sure if it was the rum from the doctor, or the devil that finally persuaded me to sign the birth certificate, but I did. I signed it.

"Stop worrying Mr. Pasden. Everything will work out. You'll see."

"I do worry. I know my daughter is bald now, but I don't want my daughter's birth certificate to say she's a boy."

"Mr Pasden, I can see you are stressed. Getting stressed will give you a headache. Would you like some more rum, or would you prefer me giving you a massage? Both will help you relax."

"That's OK. If I get a headache I'll just call a witch doctor... I mean I'll just take an aspirin."

Making it back to the hospital room, I find Rose awake holding our baby girl. Aprilynn coos. I smile and Rose smiles back. It's my beautiful family. At this moment, nothing else in the world seems to matter. At least not tonight...

... But tomorrow is a different matter.

Early the next morning, breakfast is served. I eat. Rose eats. But Aprilynn... well, she doesn't want to nurse from Rose.

"I don't know why she doesn't want to nurse from me. Can you ask the nurse for a bottle? Maybe she'll like that instead."

Minutes later the nurse arrives. "Here's a bottle for your baby and here's Aprilynn's birth certificate.

Make sure you check it over. If you see a mistake, let us know."

As Rose feeds Aprilynne, I look over the birth certificate and I immediately I see a mistake. Then I see another mistake. So before the nurse gets down the hall I call her back. "Excuse me. There are two mistakes. Big mistakes. First, our daughter's name is misspelled. It's supposed to be 'Aprilynn' not 'Aprilynne'. Second, I'm an American, but it says on the birth certificate that I'm Filipino."

"Don't worry. It can be fixed."

"Great. When your done, bring me the corrected copy so I can proofread it."

"Oh Sir, we don't make the corrections here in the hospital. After we put it on the birth certificate, then it becomes an official document. *We* can't change it here, so you'll need to hire an attorney. Then the attorney can have it changed. Would you like the name of the attorney who can do this? He does this all the time."

"Are these people kidding me? Hire their attorney?" Needless to say, I refuse take the attorney's information. Instead I just want to scream, but I've already witnessed what happens when someone screams at a hospital. Instead I ask, "Is there a witch doctor in the house? I need someone to make me a voodoo doll."

Instead of getting the voodoo doll, I kiss Rose, the baby, and I immediately leave the hospital to see our personal attorney.

Entering our attorney's office, I immediately explain the whole story to him. Even the part about them having me sign blank forms. He laughs, and assures me this is a common error that happens to all the foreigners who have babies in the Philippines He also assures me it can easily be fixed and not to worry.

"Don't worry Mr Pasden. I will fix the problem. Her name will be spelled correctly and she will be a Filipino-American. Then she can be a Filipino citizen and an American citizen."

Instantly a sensation of relief washes over me. "Thanks Ernie. That's what I needed to hear."

"Now, Mr Pasden, all I need from you is for you to sign these forms."

I look at the forms, and instantly I go from calm to irate. "Ernie, are you kidding me? These forms are blank too!"

"Don't worry. I do this all the time. Trust me. I'm a professional."

"That's exactly what the hospital said!"

He laughs and slides the form in front of me again. "Please sign... And by the way, I need $1000 too."

With my blood boiling, I'm seriously thinking of contacting Rose's grandfather.

"Ernie, before I sign this, I need something from you. And no questions."

"Of course Mr Pasden. What is it?"

"Don't worry. I only need a clipping of your hair..."

Beach Life

One of the more memorable things my parents did for me as a child, was taking me to the beach each year. We'd play in the sand, swim in the surf, explore for treasure and watch the magical sunsets. Our beach vacations not only gave us adventure and excitement, they also gave us the opportunity to bond and get to know each other as friends.

Now that I'm a parent, I'm hoping to do the same with Aprilynn. And since we only live a few hours from the beach, why not start creating those childhood experiences now while she is a baby?

"Hurray, we are going to the beach! I love the beach. I remember when I was a little girl, we'd wake up before the sunrise and we'd start walking. And when the sun was just beginning to set would be about the time we would be arriving at the beach. We'd build a fire, we'd sing songs, and we'd sleep on the sand. The next morning we'd catch pretty peesh, we'd play in the surf, and we'd sing. It was so much fun! Greg, thank you for taking us to the beach. Now Aprilynn can enjoy the ocean too."

As always, Rose is very energetic. But today she is more energetic because yesterday she graduated from nursing school and today we are celebrating at the beach.

"I'm bringing sunblock for April and you. Both of you are very white. Your pale skin will easily burn in the sun. Hopefully one day April will have beautiful dark skin like me."

"Thanks Hon. I didn't realize our pale white skin wasn't pretty," I tease.

Aside from being energetic, Rose is super organized. Last night I didn't have to do a thing to get us prepared for our beach trip. She packed the car with diapers, our clothes and necessary supplies. All I had to do was sing April to sleep. From my perspective, I think I got the better deal.

"Let's get in the car. I'm ready for the beach. Greg, can you carry April to the car? I would carry her too but I'm carrying the cooler of drinks."

We'd be going to the beach more often, but unfortunately, we live 3 hours away. Also the public beaches are packed on the weekends with everyone fleeing the crowded cities. So to avoid the beach invasion this weekend, I'm taking the girls to a secluded resort where we'll have our own private beach. Rose deserves the luxury of privacy, and this will allow us to have a more intimate family experience.

After arriving at the resort, the bellmen takes our belongings to our room, and we immediately change into our swimsuits. After a slathering of sunblock 1 million, we head straight to the beach.

The talcum white sand, the gentle breeze blowing through the palm trees, and the tranquil sound of the waves are making me feel like I'm living in paradise.

"Honey ko, being on the beach is perfect. I wish we could do this everyday. It's a great way for us to bond while enjoying the simple sensations of togetherness on the beach."

As soon as those words came out of Rose's mouth, it was like a magical incantation. April gets up on her hands and knees and begins crawling in the sand toward the sea.

"Look Greg, look! April is crawling! I think she loves this beach lifestyle too. Crawl baby, crawl!"

"Rose I think April crawling in the sand is a sign. Maybe we should make your wish come true. I mean be on the beach everyday. Maybe we can make it a reality. Why should we stay in Angeles City? The Philippines is a beautiful country with over 7100 islands. I'm sure we can find an island in the sun where we can do this everyday. What do you say?"

"Really? You mean it?"

"Yes, I really mean it. I've been thinking... We only live once, so I want our family to grow up and enjoy *life*. I want us to have fun everyday. I want to make memories that will last a life time. I want us to wake up everyday and say, 'I love our life in paradise'. And I think raising our family on a little island in the sun, near the beach, will be a great adventure. What do you say?"

"I say Yes! Let's do it! When can we start?"

"Let's enjoy watching April crawl on the beach for another 3 days. Then we'll worry about finding our slice of paradise — our tropical island in the sun, with lots of palm trees, cool ocean breezes, and our toes enjoying the warm, talcum white sand. We can start each morning with a sunrise walk on the beach. Then we can spend a few hours riding the waves. After that we'll have breakfast with the local fishermen on the beach. We'll be eating fresh fish, fruit and drinking rich coffee while listening to the wild life in the nearby jungle. In the afternoon we'll try snorkeling followed by an outdoor shower under a waterfall so we can feel the warm sun on us while enjoying the view of the ocean. In the evening we'll grill on an open fire. Then April, you and I will spend the evening laying on the beach near the fire. We'll look at the stars, listen to the ocean, share stories, and be happy."

"You sound like you've already been there."

"I have, but only in my mind."

"It sounds like Paradise, and a place where we can have many adventures. Do you think a place like this really exists?"

"I do. Now it's your turn to trust me."

"I trust you completely. Let's start planning. Let's start looking. When are we going to this new paradise?"

"I'll take you there very soon... in the next book - ***Good Morning from Paradise***"

Thank you for reading Like Winning the Lottery - How Moving to an Island Paradise made me Happier than a Millionaire & How I'm Loving Life as an Expat.

I hope you enjoyed reading the book as much as I did writing it.

Could I ask you a favor? If you enjoyed the book, would you mind writing a kind review the book on amazon.com. I'd really appreciate a 5 or a 4 star rating :-)

If you can't rate at 5 stars, then let me know on my Facebook page www.facebook.com/likewinningthelottery and we can chat about it - I'd like to make the next book even better.

Thanks again, and we hope to see you here in the sun.
Sincerely,
Greg Pasden
Other links:
www.facebook.com/goodmorningfromparadise
www.goodmorningfromparadise.com

Acknowledgments

I'd like to thank the following people for helping me make this book come true.

Thank you Chris and Theresa Fajilan Bech for helping us find our place in the sun on this fantastic tropical island in paradise, for being great neighbors and for helping us promote this book through their national newspaper, *The Boracay Sun*.

To Nadine Hays, author of *Happier Than a Billionaire*, for encouraging me during the stressful writing and editing phases — thanks for the push when I needed a boost.

To Cj Small - thanks for the motivation.

To Denise Ackerly for helping me edit my first edition so I could publish this edition.

To our Facebook friends and family who pushed me to finish — instead of letting me spend more time playing in the sun.

And most of all I would like to thank my wonderful wife Rose. Because everyday you make me so happy. So much so that I need to pinch myself to remind me that I'm not dreaming while we are enjoying our happy lives in paradise.

Join Us
www.GoodMorningFromParadise.com

Made in the USA
Coppell, TX
22 February 2021

50661741R00075